*Critical Approaches*
*to the Writings of Juan Benet*

# Critical Approaches
# to the Writings of Juan Benet

edited by
ROBERTO C. MANTEIGA,
DAVID K. HERZBERGER,
and
MALCOLM ALAN COMPITELLO

Foreword by JUAN BENET

 Published for University of Rhode Island
by University Press of New England
Hanover and London, 1984

UNIVERSITY PRESS OF NEW ENGLAND

BRANDEIS UNIVERSITY

BROWN UNIVERSITY

CLARK UNIVERSITY

DARTMOUTH COLLEGE

UNIVERSITY OF NEW HAMPSHIRE

UNIVERSITY OF RHODE ISLAND

TUFTS UNIVERSITY

UNIVERSITY OF VERMONT

Printed in the United States of America

LIBRARY OF CONGRESS CATALOGING IN PUBLICATION DATA
Main entry under title:

Critical approaches to the writings of Juan Benet.

   Bibliography: p.
   Includes index.
   1. Benet, Juan—Criticism and interpretation—
Addresses, essays, lectures.   I. Manteiga, Roberto C.
II. Herzberger, David K.   III. Compitello, Malcolm Alan,
1946–   .   IV. University of Rhode Island.
PQ6652.E5Z59   1984        863'.64        83-40010
ISBN 0-87451-270-0

The authors wish to thank the University of Rhode Island and the University of Connecticut for grants that made the publication of this book possible. Grateful acknowledgment is made to *The American Hispanist* for permission to reprint essays by Esther Nelson and Stephen J. Summerhill.

The publisher is appreciative of support from the University of Connecticut for the publication of this book.

# Contents

# Foreword

Whether or not one agrees with what others say, it is always disquieting to read something written about one's own work. In principle, a critic's study of a literary work can be of interest to all readers, with the exception of the author of that work; for what can be said about it that the author did not know beforehand? Who better than he knows its intention and meaning—be it explicit or implicit, its style, its narrative technique, its relation to his own experiences, the cultural environment in which it was engendered, the influences that decisively molded its coming into being? Unless one agrees that an author is basically unaware of his work, or capable of writing it in a state of literary semiconsciousness, one ought to recognize that all critical endeavors constitute only a disciplinary approximation to a reality that only the author knows fully. An analogy to judicial proceedings is not completely metaphorical: society entrusts the critic to investigate the causes and, above all, the nature of an act perpetrated by the author, which the latter—having confessed his guilt—refuses to discuss. In a certain sense one can say that such a trust is impelled by a spirit and intention completely opposed to that which originally inspired the author to write his work. Indeed, the present volume of essays "is intended to help the reader penetrate Benet's fiction and theory well beyond page fifteen," as is stated in the preface. Leaving aside the humanitarian aspect (which I believe is not relevant here) that such assistance represents, for the reader as well as for me, such an intention inexorably leads me to ask, once again, what can be the value of a literary work that resists being read beyond page fifteen? I suppose that if it lacks value, the best thing the critic can do is to silence the work. But if the work indeed has value, is it a question of hidden value that can be appreciated only with outside help? If my work is so entangled that the average reader needs a mentor in or-

der to penetrate it, why didn't I, at the time of writing it, draw upon
that mentor or, better yet, with a bit more effort, why didn't I em-
bark on the path of clarifying it and making it accessible to the
average reader and, at the same time, try to preserve its value as
much as possible? Or would solving the enigmas and eliminating
the difficulties be a vain and counterproductive effort that would
ruin that possible value? Finally, may it be that value, enigma, and
difficulty are indissolubly united in that work of fiction?

In the first place, I must say that if I have not been clearer—in
any sentence, paragraph, or page of my fiction—it is because I have
been unable to be so. What I have said, even of an obscure nature, I
have said in the clearest possible way that was in my power. To have
done otherwise—by introducing unnecessary obscurity in a gra-
tuitous fashion, simply to mortify the reader, or to hide a scarcely
relevant text in chiaroscuro—would have been to go against my
own interests or, at least, to undermine my beliefs and allow myself
the literary vices that I detest. Having rather few clear ideas and, for
the most part, not knowing how to resolve the enigmas, I can think
of no worse enterprise than to becloud darkness.

Hence—it will be said—my work demands mentors; persons
who, thanks to hours of study and dedication, will help others get
through it, eliminating obstacles and illuminating dark corners. But
even if my work were not as it is, these persons would be necessary.
One of the great advantages of the critic over the narrator is that he
works on a specific field, on a discrete entity, where he can make use
of general principles as well as those of a particular science. The
critic does not speak of anger in general, but rather of the anger of
Achilles, with the facts supplied by Homer. As a result, he can arrive at a descriptive formulation of that particularized emotion in
an individual who, no doubt, eludes Homer as well as the psycholo-
gist. Because of that he does not stop doing science. On the contrary, he broadens it in its most modern dimension: detail.

JUAN BENET
NEW YORK CITY, MARCH 1982

# Preface

Juan Benet falls chronologically into the group of writers commonly known as the Generation of 1950. Benet's early works of fiction appeared at a time in Spain when social realistic narrative emerged as the predominant literary mode. During this period Benet formed personal friendships with many of the writers of his generation and published his first work (*Max*, 1953) in *Revista Española*, a short-lived literary outlet for several young writers who would later become respected advocates of the social novel. Despite his literary milieu, however, Benet never embraced the underlying principles of social realism. Even in his earliest short stories it is clear that he favored a brand of writing more attuned to an extraordinary personal vision than to the literary trends of the moment. Indeed, his recognition as a distinguished writer during the past decade can be traced in large part to the uniqueness of his literary posture, to his rejection of social realism, and to the complexity of ideas and narrative forms that he offers in its place.

Benet's fiction rarely permits us to feel at ease. After finishing a work, we are left with the disquieting thought that we have missed the point, or that there are many more points than we could possibly imagine—or worse yet, that there is no point at all. Benet's works challenge us to rethink critical traditions that demand decisive meanings or that wrest from our analysis unresolved ambiguities. Indeed, Benet impels the critical enterprise to the limits of pluralism perhaps more than any writer of postwar Spain—not merely because of the richness of his ideas, but because of the density of his texts and the intricate webwork of his language.

Complex, difficult, enigmatic—these and like adjectives have been the weapons wielded both by those seeking to praise and, at times, to condemn Benet. Few would argue that Benet's works are easily penetrated, and readers have on occasion turned away from them in nonplussed frustration. As one Spanish critic has written, "I am certain that a novel by Juan Benet is very good, but I have as yet been unable to get past page fifteen." Certainly, complexity of thought cannot assure originality of insight, just as stylistic intricacy is no guarantee of literary value. But neither should difficulty and abstruseness deter the reader from his or her critical task. Indeed, for the committed reader, the effort is rewarding.

It is in this spirit of inquiry that this volume of essays is offered: to help the reader penetrate Benet's fiction and theory well beyond page fifteen. Although we have not included studies on each of Benet's individual works, we have covered much critical ground by selecting essays that probe his literary theory, short stories, and novels. While the essays cannot be linked by a common methodological or theoretical posture, the emphasis in each is on the texts that Benet has produced rather than on Benet the writer who stands behind his texts. These studies scrutinize Benet's writings at close range, and it is our hope that they afford a lucid and penetrating portrait of Benet's literary vision.

We wish to make it clear, however, that the essays of this collection are by no means advanced as unquestionable truths concerning Benet's writing; on the contrary, the diversity of critical perspectives provides varying and sometimes contradictory explanations. Hence we have not endeavored to make the reader feel completely at home in the world of Juan Benet, but rather have sought to open the door and explore the areas of his writing rich and complex in their polysemy, and thereby inviting and challenging.

*Critical Approaches*
*to the Writings of Juan Benet*

ROBERT C. SPIRES

# Juan Benet's Poetics of Open Spaces

Juan Benet's emergence on the Spanish literary scene in the 1960s
was greeted with acclaim tempered by a tone of barely disguised
irritation. Critics had enough problems trying to explain the linguistic and structural innovations of novelists like Martín-Santos
and Juan Goytisolo without having the further difficulty of clarifying the "blatantly contrived obfuscations" of Benet. In effect, only
recently have critics recognized as futile and counterproductive any
attempt to solve the plot enigmas of Benet's novels; the enigmas are
irreconcilable contradictions challenging the very concept of novelistic representation. This challenge to representation, whether an-
ticipating or merely echoing current poststructuralist thought, is
Benet's major contribution to the novelistic innovations ushered
into Spain by the new novel of the 1960s. Before attempting to
define more fully the nature of his challenge, it is useful to take
a brief backward glance at the concept of representation in respect
to neorealism and to the Martín-Santos/Goytisolo school of the
new novel.

The neorealism of the first two decades of postwar Spain is characterized by the use of predominantly referential language. The
novels assigned to this category tend to foreground a mimetic representation of reality, that is, they feature familiar objects, people,
and places photographically represented. The unfortunate result of
this realistic mode is that many critics read these novels as mere
documents, ignoring the fact that art always strives to transcend

mimesis by creating a structure of meaning beyond the objects to which it refers. For example, the structure of meaning in *La familia de Pascual Duarte* evolves primarily from the various levels of narration. In the case of *Nada*, the distinction between the narrating self and the experiencing self is central to the novel's message. In both *El Jarama* and *Los bravos*, the personification of nature plays a key role in the novels' structure of meaning. Notwithstanding these nonmimetic dimensions, all the works mentioned placed so much emphasis on mimetic representation as a point of departure that all too often the transcending structure of meaning was ignored, and readers' comments tended to focus on the relative verisimilitude of this or that scene, character, or episode. As a result, the novelists' inevitable reaction was toward a more nonrepresentational mode, or what is commonly labeled the Spanish new novel of the 1960s and early 1970s.

The new novel's reaction against the dominance of representation, a reaction initiated by the publication of *Tiempo de silencio* in 1962, generally takes the form of self-referential language. Whereas the language of neorealism may be said to be transparent, since the reader tends to look through it directly at the represented object, the language of the new novel is opaque: the reader does not look through, but at it. An example of such self-referential language is a neologism. When confronted with a neologism, the reader must focus on the word itself in order to decipher its phonic-semantic roots and, from these, its cultural codes. This technique of foregrounding language itself, though certainly a reaction against representation, still reflects a basic faith in the direct relationship between the signifier and the signified. In other words, in novels such as *Señas de identidad, Don Julián, Parábola del náufrago, Oficio de tinieblas 5, Agata, ojo de gato, La saga/fuga de J.B.*, and others, there is the implication that a proper decoding of the word will lead the reader directly to reality. Juan Benet, on the other hand, adds a significant dimension to the new novel not only by foregrounding language, but by systematically negating any direct relationship between the signifier and the signified. Rather than leading the reader from the word directly to the real object, Benet forces him into the open space beyond words and objects where preconscious experiences are stored, an open space he sometimes calls a "zona de sombras."

Critics have been quick to note various stylistic characteristics of Benet's novels that, to paraphrase the prevailing reaction, leave the reader in the dark. Among the most commonly mentioned techniques contributing to confusion are an excessively elaborate, almost Germanic syntax, page-long sentences, the complete absence of paragraph and chapter divisions (as in the case of *Una meditación*), a highly technical vocabulary, character-narrators who border on lunacy, the fusion of various narrative voices, and of course the contradictions in plot. But whereas all these techniques reflect Benet's poetics, his essays provide a more direct access to the theoretical bases underlying the techniques. I turn, therefore, to two of his collections of essays published in 1976—*En ciernes* and *El ángel del Señor abandona a Tobías*[1]—in a tentative effort to establish the conceptual framework of his perplexing artistic creations. I want to emphasize the word tentative, however, since even in his expository writing Benet seems to revel in the prospect of leading his reader into the nearly impenetrable "zonas de sombras." The path I chart to lead us into and, I hope, out of this shadowy zone will guide us through Benet's concepts of scientific knowledge, duality, contradiction, and preconscious experience as they relate to language and reality, a relationship ultimately defined by the open spaces between the word and the object.

At the core of Benet's artistic philosophy are a skepticism of scientific knowledge and an outright rejection of what he considers the pseudoscientific claims of linguistics, structuralism, and semiotics: "Participo de la creencia de que el lenguaje es absolutamente irreductible a la ciencia" (*Tobías*, p. 148). In fact, all scientific investigations, he claims, merely reveal their own limitations; their advances only enable us to see more clearly the nothingness just over the horizon: "Tal vez el máximo representante de la ciencia sea aquel que ha visto que más allá del presunto avance de las luces no hay nada, no hay logos, no hay otra cosa que el precario y limitado recinto de una pragmática humana que a su mejor entender resuelve su puesto en el universo a conciencia de que nunca dará con la cifra del mismo" (*Tobías*, p. 191). Such a statement echoes the poststructuralists' rejection of the semioticians' logocentric view of the universe, or a view that absolute meaning stems from a central and divine source. According to Benet, all words are tentative and in constant battle with the objects they attempt to portray precisely because there is no central source of language. The novelist, therefore, must recognize both the limitations and the potential of the words he uses: "La lección salta a la vista: sólo la ambigüedad tiene capacidad para hacer historia. Y es la lucha la que ha enriquecido semánticamente (las palabras); basta una mirada superficial al diccionario etimológico para advertir como el giro y el ensanchamiento semántico proceden, de una u otra manera, si no de la disputa al menos de la pugna" (*Tobías*, p. 56). Benet incorporates into his novels his conviction that ambiguity, rather than illusory clarity, is the only authentic means by which art can convey reality through the use of contrasting dualities.

The novelistic technique of contrasting dualities reflects not only Benet's concept of language, but what he sees as an essential premise of all religions: "Aquí cabe añadir que incluyendo todas las concepciones religiosas monistas, incluyendo el zervanismo iranio anterior a esa doble divinidad que emana de un solo Dios, la idea más simple de Dios introduce sin más ni más el dualismo, al establecer claramente dos campos, el humano y el divino" (*Tobías*, p. 124). He feels, therefore, that this duality inherent to human existence imposes itself one way or another on the novelist: "gran parte del discurso literario no sería posible si no se desarrollara entre el espacio abierto . . . entre una afirmación y su correspondiente negación" (*Ciernes*, p. 52). Benet seems to be saying that meaning is conveyed by a structure of differences: the word does not tell us what its referent is, but rather what it is not. In order to underscore this inherent difference between language and reality, Benet relies on the use of contrast: "a veces dos discursos diferentes, cada uno de los cuales arrastra su propia lógica, su mecanismo asociativo y su cadena de ideas, chocan como dos ondas de distinta polaridad para producir en su recíproca fisión la partícula que consume, reúne y amplifica la energía de ambas trayectorias" (*Tobías*, p. 122). The concept of infusing new energy into language by means of a structure of difference is also implicit in Benet's definition of a metaphor: the use of an object or concept in such a context that it must refer to something other than itself. The structure of difference between the linguistic marker and the object to which it refers frees language from a univocal reading; the contrast leads us to the open space between word and concept. Yet the very act of reading and interpreting is in eternal conflict with the energizing effect of contrasting dualities. As we read and interpret we inevitably attempt to close the open spaces created by the dualities; we feel the need to fuse word and object, sign and meaning.

To counteract the tendency toward closure inherent in the reading and interpreting process, Benet relies on contradiction, a device he considers the artist's "fuente de estímulos e inspiración" (*Ciernes*, p. 51). The most striking use of contradictions in Benet's novels involves the plots themselves. Whether it be a case of one narrator contradicting himself or of several narrators contradicting one another, it becomes impossible to arrive at a definitive summary of the plots. As the story is told, it is as if the initial version of the action were inadequate, and thus another version must be offered, which also proves inadequate, and so on. Since the novelist plants a series of "miswritings," as readers we participate in a series of "misreadings" without ever arriving at an authoritative or correct reading of the events. Consequently our tendency to close the open spaces between contradictory versions is frustrated, and we are forced to accept the work on its own polysemic terms. Stated in another way, the contradictions themselves function as signs, which, though pointing toward the familiar themes of chaos, despair, decadence, timelessness, and death, resist our efforts to impose a univocal meaning on them. In short, the technique of plot contradictions is a dramatic demonstration of Benet's thesis that language is by definition "un continuo pluridimensional, nunca una representación ni un registro" (*Tobías*, p. 82). And the essential element of language's plural dimension is the inevitable difference between the author's and the reader's experiences, a difference that can be resolved only in the shadowy zone of the preconscious.

Preconscious experiences, finally, form the nucleus of Benet's theories on language, literature, and reality. Word and object can never become one because the very act of naming triggers a chain reaction

transcending the powers of mere reason: "nada más obvio que . . .
el elemento nuclear que da forma a memoria y lenguaje—el vehículo de formulación de la temporalidad—sea ese residuo factual,
vestigio de una conducta instintiva, que pone en íntima y autónoma
relación—no dependiente del contraste intelectivo—la función sen-
sorial cenestésica con el movimiento de la vida dentro de las dimensiones no-espirituales del continuo" (*Tobías*, p. 84). No matter how
concrete the object may seem to be, any attempt to describe it lin-
guistically will result in a multidimensional image; every object is
marked by an invisible trace ("vestigio") of human experiences pre-
dating the sender's and the receiver's consciousness, yet triggering
their multiple instinctive reactions. Because of our contemporary
obsession with scientific explanations, however, there is a tendency
to suppress what cannot be quantified in supposedly absolute
terms: in other words, to suppress our instinctive reaction to language. Benet is intent on reaffirming the role of instinct. As we
struggle through his novels from one ambiguous discourse to another, from one contrast to another, and from one contradiction to
another, we inevitably end up in an open space or "zona de sombras" where mankind's accumulated experiences are stored. Benet's
poetics, therefore, is designed to take us beyond objects and words
—beyond representation—to those open spaces where we may become more acutely aware of our own role in the multidimensional
continuum of human existence. Benet, trained as an engineer,
writes novels designed to reject science for what he terms a "pre-
ciencia y metaciencia" of preconscious experiences (*Tobías*, p. 80).

I began this essay with an attempt to define how Benet's challenge
to representation signifies a unique contribution to novelistic innovation of the new novel of the 1960s and early 1970s. I would also
like to say a word concerning his link with the type of metafiction
that emerged in the second half of the seventies. Novels such as
*Juan sin Tierra, Los verdes de mayo hasta el mar, Fragmentos de
apocalipsis, La cólera de Aquiles*, and several others represent not
only self-conscious narration, but they also foreground their own
process of becoming novels; they are, or at least propose to be, their
own referents. This culmination of a general process in Spanish
postwar fiction of turning the narration inward on itself strikes me

as a logical extension of Benet's attempt to lead us away from a direct and absolute word-object, sign-concept relationship. He was the first postwar Spanish novelist to practice consciously and to theorize persuasively about the inherent differences between language and reality. Finally, I would like to clarify that my purpose has not been that of defending Benet as a novelist, but rather to suggest a new way to read, or in deference to poststructuralist terminology, to misread, his novels and even his essays.

MALCOLM ALAN COMPITELLO

# The Paradoxes of Praxis:
# Juan Benet and Modern Poetics

During the past decade, Juan Benet has built a solid reputation as a
literary theorist and critic. Yet it remains an aspect of his work that
has received scant critical attention.[1] Out of step with current
trends in both literature and criticism, Benet's remarks have been
considered mere verbal histrionics on more than one occasion.[2] Behind these often controversial statements, however, lies an inter-
nally coherent and meticulously elaborated viewpoint that informs
his literary judgments. Still, certain enigmatic seams are perceptible
in this well-wrought theoretical construct. The first is the paradox
of his rejection of prevalent working models of literary and linguistic analysis even though his own praxis as a critic approaches, on a
number of important issues, the types of critical and theoretical activity he assails. The second is the paradoxical distance between
Benet's theoretical and creative praxis, especially in the way the latter articulates relationships between literature and society that are
silenced in his theoretical statements. My purpose here is to demonstrate the most interesting of these contradictions: the points of
confluence between the Spanish writer's views on literature and
those of French structuralism and Russian formalism, two critical
modes rejected by Benet in his own texts. I shall also suggest how to
assess that gap between the writer's view of novel writing and his
own narrative fiction.

Benet's most strident condemnation of modern poetics is found in his reply to a survey on literature in the Spanish educational system:

Observe si no el ejemplo de la crítica más contemporánea que nos llega de Francia y América—y que tantos adeptos está encontrando en nuestro país—y dígame si no despide toda ella el tufillo de los escolásticos abstemios, casi exclusivamente preocupados en la búsqueda del método. Partiendo de aquella privilegiada e intemporal situación posterior a toda literatura la crítica se cierra sobre sí misma y se sustenta de ella misma, sin necesidad de nutrirse de las letras y librada de aquella denigrante condición parasitaria. Con residuo de aquel vínculo servil ya sólo quedan unos pocos sentimientos porque una vez emancipada aspira sustituirla. De la misma manera que la ciencia, tras desmontar a la religión para cuyo servicio nació, ha reclamado para sí los adeptos y los procedimientos de obediencia de aquella, la moderna crítica pretenderá ser la depositaria del saber y del apetito literarios, relegando a la literatura al papel de mero vehículo para alcanzar esta meta. La verdadera aspiración de la crítica moderna no será por consiguiente explicar la literatura, sino sustituirla.[3]

While I do not subscribe completely to his point of view, there is an element of truth in his argument. Clearly, certain critical modes, especially in the hands of the inept, do occasionally become an end in and of themselves.[4] More important is the fact that this statement synthesizes the paradoxical tension that I wish to explore, and, by so doing, provides an excellent point of departure for my remarks. Benet's comments are in perfect consonance with his view of the self-sufficiency of literary art. Hence the critique of modes that undermine that status should bear a close resemblance to his own literary position.

Far and above the most important element of Benet's ideas is the insistence that literature be understood on its own terms as a self-regulating system. Approaches that circumscribe the almost "mystical" space Benet reserves for the creative process, or that attempt to calibrate it scientifically, draw his scorn; he especially dislikes systems whose hypotheses are sociologically mediated. Benet declared the necessity of understanding literature on its own terms during his well-publicized and controversial participation in a round-table discussion on the novel almost a decade ago.[5] When asked what he considered an adequate "proyecto literario" he responded in the following manner.

Un proyecto literario centrado sobre las artes narrativas y sobre las reglas del arte literario que no se definan por otras clausuras de la sociedad. ¿Existe un arte literario? ¿Existen unas reglas del arte literario? ¿Existen unos progresos del arte literario, una evolución de este arte literario? Lo sociológico no es lo determinante, no es lo que marca la historia del arte literario; el arte literario está marcado por lo concreto, porque un señor produce un salto de aquí a allá y otro lo hace retroceder, etc. (p. 50)

In opposition to a sociologically mediated view of literary history, evolution, and creation, Benet consistently sees literature as a semi-autonomous, self-regulating system governed by a few basic principles. The most important of these are the two mentioned in the title of his collection of essays *La inspiración y el estilo.*[6]

Inspiration provides the author with his working material, while style is the instrumentality through which inspiration is expressed. The author who is incapable of developing and dominating a style is destined to mediocrity. Furthermore, the relationship between inspiration and style is symbiotic: the former provides the glimmer of an idea that the writer elaborates through the medium of the latter. Once a style is fully developed, however, the relationship between the two becomes so intimate that inspiration not only functions within the style developed by the author, but also impels its eventual course.[7]

The end product of the union of style and inspiration is a literary work whose most important constituent elements are style and information: "el escritor acostumbra a sostener entre sus dedos dos hilos heterogéneos, cada uno de los cuales le conduce a una fuente de interés diferente: la información y el estilo. El primero existe, es palpable, se puede decir que salta a la vista; el segundo es quizá nada más que una añaganza; en ese sentido el estilo no es más que un esfuerzo del escritor por superar el interés intrínseco de la información para extraer de ella su naturaleza caediza y confeccionarle otra perdurable" (*Inspiración*, p. 138). Style is given primacy since it "detemporalizes" the information in such a way as to secure its lasting value as literature.

The style/information relationship is not be be confused with the traditional form/content dichotomy underlying most modes of literary analysis. Style and information are inextricably linked; form

and content are not, paradoxically, because they cannot be separated in the first place. Attempts to do so are born from the idea
that the same content can be expressed in many different forms
without substantially altering the nature of that content. Benet,
however, clearly rejects this notion. Every modification in the form
(the signifier) alters the content embodied in that form (the signified). The form/content dichotomy is odious, therefore, because it
fails to recognize a fundamental element of literary construction.[8]

Chance occurrence provides Benet's alternative to a predictable
sociologically mediated process of literary evolution. External
agents do not create genius, nor can theories based on such factors
predict its occurrence; only chance can. "El azar produjo tres novelistas de altura universal en los Estados Unidos en los años veinte;
fue un azar y no un movimiento sociológico. Movimiento sociológico es el movimiento francés que trata de extraer con un ém-
bolo buena literatura y no lo ha logrado; y pueden inventar lo que
se quiera. Luego, sin que nadie se lo proponga, saldrá en el sudoeste
de Francia un novelista que sí, será un verdadero novelista. Y no
será el *ancien roman* o el *nouveau roman*, sino el azar."[9] The insistence on the role of chance in enhancing the predictability of literary achievement is related to Benet's insistence on "taste," both at
the creative and appreciative levels.

Artistic appreciation cannot be taught, nor can it be reduced to
a scientific formula. Insight comes with time and to those who
surround themselves with literature. Only from such an immersion
can an appreciation of it emerge. Creativity, therefore, is also irreducible to simple formulas.[10] Efforts to categorize the creative and
appreciative processes are exemplified by *la novelística* vilified by
Benet on every available occasion. The latter establishes parameters, categories into which one places literature (here fiction), and
therefore stands at the opposite end of the spectrum from the artist,
whose goal is to create something the very nature of which lies outside the boundaries circumscribed by categories. The aim of the artist is the exploration through his art of a created second reality, a
system of representations as Benet labels it.[11] Thus the dialectical
relationship between that product of his style and the information
he draws on to shape it ultimately expands the horizons of both

reader and writer. "Y cuando esas reglas del juego, o ese instru-
mento, sirven para profundizar el conocimiento de la primera realidad, tanto mejor. En definitiva, la literatura, lo único que hace es
investigar, crear una segunda realidad, y, por su parecido con la primera, profundizar en el conocimiento de la primera." [12]

With the main components of Benet's idea of literature predi-
cated on purely literary values, his view of its self-referentiality is
coherent and intelligible if judged from his own perspective—although many observers may find it unacceptable. What is more,
this belief renders completely understandable Benet's abhorrence of
"sciences of literature." Literary sociologists are the ilk that Benet
has criticized most frequently. On one occasion he went so far, although with what degree of seriousness it is difficult to say, as to
label them frustrated scientists looking for an area to exercise their
training. [13] Underlying his distaste is the fear that sociology can per-
vert literature by exhalting second-rate figures in the name of sociological importance. This type of literature, labeled *costum-
brismo*, attempts a critical assessment of its own ambience through
a faithful portrayal of the surface manifestations of that reality. It
fails because it delves no deeper than that surface and is condemned
precisely because of its poor quality as art. For this reason, when
sociological conditions change, it is doomed to be forgotten,
shelved as sociological information pertaining to a bygone era, of
less value than historical documents for reconstructing the conditions of its period.

It becomes apparent to anyone familiar with the development of
modern poetics that in many respects Benet's critical praxis is very
close to the modes he scorns. The key to these paradoxical affinities
lies in the role played by Russian formalism and French structuralism, and to a lesser extent, semiotics, in establishing new bases for
the study of literature. The first advance that modern poetics
wrought in the field of literary analysis was in establishing what literary studies should do, that is to say, defining their theoretical objective. Reacting against the positivistic works of their predeces-
sors, the formalists sought to establish literary studies as an
autonomous scientific discipline whose object would be to study
the "literariness" of literary discourse (that is, those elements that

differentiate a literary text from other types of discourse). The question now posed in relation to the literary text no longer centers on
the meaning of its content, nor on its emergence in literary history,
but on the art of its construction. The latter became the central element in the formalists' definition of literature. In this light, it is interesting to compare the now famous assessment by Roman Jakob-
son of the change in the literary arena wrought by formalist
scholarship with Benet's views examined above.

The object of study in literary science is not literature but "literariness,"
that is, what makes a given work a "literary" work. Meanwhile, the situation has been that the historian of literature acts like nothing so much as a
policeman, who, out to arrest a certain culprit, takes into custody (just in
case) everything and everyone that they [*sic*] find at the scene as well as any
passers-by for good measure. The historians of literature helped themselves
to everything—environment, psychology, politics, philosophy. Instead of a
science of literature, they have worked up a concoction of home-made disciplines. They seem to have forgotten that those subjects pertain to their
own fields of study—to the history of philosophy, the history of culture,
psychology, and so on, and that those fields of study certainly may utilize
literary monuments as documents of a defective and second-class variant
among other materials.[14]

There is a striking similarity between the way Benet and Jakob-
son capture the essence of literature and literary study. Both insist
that literature be judged on its own terms, on that which is specifically literary in it, while at the same time rejecting as inadequate
extrinsically oriented approaches. While Benet might pale at having
his work compared to a view of literature that wished to establish
itself as a science, the rigor involved in the conceptualization of
viewpoints in both cases is imposing, as is their mutual desire to
break with antecedent and contemporary formulations both within
their own contexts and within the broader sphere of literary studies
in general.

Benet's views vis-à-vis the form/content and style/information relationships resemble important parts of formalist and structuralist
doctrine. Underlying the reassessment of the nature of literature by
modern poetics is the same view of the inseparability of form and
content postulated by Benet. Similarly, the formalists gave primacy
to composition over material, a position seen most clearly in Viktor

Sklovskij's contribution to formalist scholarship. His definition of art as a process of defamiliarization, the making strange (*ostranenie*) of the common and everyday objects of our existence, came to be widely accepted as a method for determining "literariness."

For Sklovskij there exists a dichotomy between the familiar and automatized materials used in the construction of a literary work and the devices the artist employs to defamiliarize this material so as to make it stand out and be noticed by the reader. In the formalist analysis of narrative this idea led to a distinction between plot and story, a two-part division of narrative syntax that, with differing terminology, has become standard in structuralist narratology. Traditionally, plot was equated with content, a set of thematic motifs. For Sklovskij, however, story refers to the basic content of a narrative construction, while plot is the story as actually put together in the narrative as processed by the reader. Plot, therefore, has been displaced from the domain of thematic concerns to compositional ones. It is as much a part of composition, of form, as is the rhyme scheme of a poem. The aesthetic process consists of building story into the plot, of defamiliarizing the familiar.[15]

Both defamiliarization and the conceptualization of plot as a compositional element resonate with Benetian constructs viewed above. His idea of style's "detemporalization" of the information of the text parallels the formalist principle of defamiliarization, which changes the familiar into the artistic. Similarly, in Benet's terms, style transforms the information of literary discourse so as to provide it with its lasting artistic value. In addition, Benet's broad view of the function of style, as opposed to the narrow perception of the role of form, is similar to Sklovskij's notion of plot: both are construed as the basic compositional elements of the literary text, those which provide its "literariness."

At the beginning of this study I cited several of Benet's comments through which he established the parameters of an adequate literary project. From those remarks, and from others he has made, it becomes clear that Benet's rejection of literary evolution and of a scientifically oriented literary history is overarched by a decidedly synchronic approach to literary progress, as opposed to the primarily diachronic ones prevalent in traditional approaches to literary history. In opting for the synchronic as dominant, Benet's stance is once again very close to the underlying tenets of modern poetics, which is based on just such a reversal of the roles of diachrony and synchrony. In the formalist postulations it was necessary to redefine the concept of literary history so as to predicate it on in-system factors: on the evolution of literature itself rather than on outside influences. Boris M. Ejxenbaum's important retrospective analysis mentions this shift as one of the most difficult theoretical problems the formalists had to resolve in constructing a science of literature: "We had to demolish those academic traditions and liquidate those tendencies in journalistic criticism. We had to pit against those forces a new concept of literary evolution and of literature itself—a concept divorced from the ideas of progress and decorous succession, from the concepts of realism and romanticism, from any material extrinsic to literature as a specific order of things." [16]

The Russian critic then proceeds to pose the problem faced by the formalists in the reassessment of literary evolution in a way that parallels Benet's idea of an adequate literary project:

Naturally, with our understanding of literary evolution as the dialectical change of forms, we do not resort to the material that occupied a central position in literary evolution to the extent that it bears a specific character, and within such limits as allows us to call it autonomous, not directly dependent on other orders of culture. In other words, we limit the factors so as not to wallow in an endless quantity of vague "connections" and "correspondences," which, in any case, cannot elucidate the evolution of literature as such. We do not incorporate into our work issues involving biography or the psychology of creativity—assuming that those problems, very serious and complex in their own right, ought to have their place in other disciplines. We are concerned with finding in evolution the features of imminent historical laws. Therefore, we leave aside whatever, from that point of view, may be said to be "fortuitous," not relevant to history. What interests us is the very process of evolution, the very dynamics of literary forms in so far as it may be observed in the facts of the past. [17]

Clearly, there is a confluence of essential intent in Benet and Ejxenbaum, as both postulate similar ways of explaining change within the realm of their respective literary constructs.

Benet's supposed negation of a social or political function for literature also demonstrates his proximity to underlying presuppositions of modern poetics.[18] Formalism and structuralism consciously ignore ideological concerns. When they do enter into literary analysis, they do so at a level of abstraction that distances them from the specificity of any given sociopolitical environment. The reasons for such a stance in both contexts arose from the felt necessity of separating the analysis of literature from approaches based on extraliterary values. While I do not share this view, it is intelligible in the context in which these perceptions were formed, in the same way that Benet's apparent disavowal of social criticism is comprehensible given the parameters of his vision of literary art. In the case of Benet, however, there is a second motivation for the rejection of social or revolutionary literature, one not as important in the formalist and structuralist contexts. He believes such literature to be untrue to its nature. Morally justifiable and correct, it is, nonetheless, poor literature, and Benet condemns it in the same uncertain terms reserved for the sociology of literature.

It is at this juncture that the second rent appears in the fabric of Benet's literary construct. As I have indicated, there are several points of convergence between his views and those of the poetic modes he attacks. At the same time, his own literary practice in some important ways contradicts his theoretical texts, establishing a second paradoxical distance in his writing: one between theory and praxis. The paradox becomes intelligible if one perceives that Benet's creative works serve as the enunciation of certain silenced elements of his critical rhetoric. The key to understanding this dysfunction between theory and practice is a correct assessment of Benet's relationship to his milieu, and his personal link to social literature.

The antipathy toward poorly written social or revolutionary literature is not equivalent to support for the political status quo, an equation Benet's critics have been too prone to make. Benet, on a number of occasions, has been ringing in his condemnation of the Francoist regime. This is especially true in his monograph ¿Qué fue la guerra civil? (Barcelona: La Gaya Ciencia, 1976), a key document for the construction of his world view that has been given scant attention by critics. Second, Benet has never said definitively that social literature was unacceptable a priori. He has, in addition, always based his comments on literary projects that failed because they were first and foremost unacceptable as literature. It is my contention that Benet would accept literature that was socially critical of its environment *if at the same time it were good literature.* Furthermore, such texts do indeed exist. They can be found in the novelist's own fiction, as exemplified by *Volverás a Región,* which is, in my estimation, the most complex and literarily challenging condemnation of Francoism produced from within Spain during the postwar period. Benet's own fictional discourse is, then, the manifestation of the unarticulated positive counterpart to the poor social literature he attacks in his theory and criticism: a combination of literature with intrinsic and enduring artistic merit and decidedly social scope. At the risk of uttering the type of *boutade* for which Benet himself is famous, it is not the objectivist nor the neorealist novel that provides an adequate model for what social literature should and can be, but Juan Benet's own *Volverás a Región.*

The purpose of this essay has not been to suggest that in Juan Benet's critical discourse can be found a conscious emulation of modern critical methods, nor to imply that the confluences between his thought and the two modes examined above somehow reduce his importance as a theorist. Instead, I have sought to reveal the paradoxical and enigmatic distance that frequently arises between what Benet says and what he does. Critical practice, paradoxically, draws him near to those modes he supposedly abhors. At the same time, his own fictional discourse seemingly contradicts elements of his theory, but ultimately can be shown to express the unpronounced positive convergence of social intent and literary art left unarticulated in his criticism. Abstruse, but not indecipherable, Benet the critic and theoretician takes on the same enigmatic qualities that many have identified with his narrative.

JANET PÉREZ

# The Rhetoric of Ambiguity

Benet's style, always distinctive, usually baroque, intricate, and hermetic, and not infrequently bewildering, has often been mentioned in passing but has received less in-depth scrutiny than have his themes, motifs, use of myth, and related elements. Like his style, Benet's rhetoric has remained unelucidated in a number of significant aspects. Inasmuch as style is traditionally a subdivision of rhetoric, the latter provides a logical point of departure, and its investigation may subsequently offer a fruitful basis for further stylistic examination and analysis. Although Benet's views on rhetoric have not been systematized and can be found scattered through his volumes of essays as well as obliquely presented from time to time in his fiction, there is nonetheless a cluster of seminal concepts to be gleaned from *La inspiración y el estilo* (which, interestingly enough, is catalogued by many libraries together with treatises on rhetoric).[1] This essay will extract certain key rhetorical principles from *La inspiración y el estilo* and attempt to situate Benet within the context of the contemporary evolution of rhetorical theory.

Although in its most superficial, formal aspect, *La inspiración y el estilo* is a collection of seven essays on diverse topics ranging from Flaubert to George Eliot to Conrad to Poe, there is a unifying concern for the titular themes and for what may be called, for lack of a better term, "desirable" literary effects. Benet argues repeatedly in favor of such effects as mystery, doubt, ambiguity, uncertainty, insinuation, incompleteness and indefiniteness. His posture is, on one hand, anticlassical (or anti-neoclassical), with a rejection of dogma, unity, and uniformity, and on the other hand (most specifically in the central chapter, "La entrada en la taberna"), "anti-costumbrista," "anti-casticista." He rejects objectivism as exemplified by Flaubert, testimonial realism, the idea of the novelist as sociologist, historian, or chronicler, and the rapprochement of the novel to journalism.

Inquiring into the nature of the creative process, Benet stresses its essential impenetrability: "Uno se pregunta por ese procedimiento que le permite acertar. Tiene que ser en todos los sentidos misterioso, manifiestamente misterioso, si gracias a él puede saber lo que es nuevo sin conocer lo viejo, saber lo que es original aun desconociendo todo lo que es común" (p. 26). Polyvalence and ambiguity lie so much at the heart of creativity that Benet has recourse to paradox to explain or elucidate inspiration:

. . . la luz de la inspiración y la luz del campo que alumbra tienen un punto de parentesco y son en cierto modo homogéneas. La naturaleza de la una está condicionada por la otra, en la medida por lo menos en que *por el hecho de ser luz son también oscuridad.* Yo no creo que la luz de la inspiración sea capaz de descubrir ningún hueco, porque la inspiración le es dada a un escritor sólo cuando posee un estilo o cuando hace suyo un estilo previo. (pp. 27–28; italics mine)

Benet suggests that having clearly defined attitudes and beliefs to communicate (that is, a "message"), may be an insuperable handicap to the writer: "el escritor empieza a depurarse a partir del momento en que . . . deja entrar una gran dosis de incertidumbre en sus opiniones y en sus doctrinas, tanto como en sus métodos de trabajo y en sus criterios estéticos se vuelve más riguroso y exigente" (p. 31). This statement is especially interesting in light of the continuing view of rhetoric, from classical to modern times, as the art of argumentation or suasion, and we shall have occasion to return to it later.

Benet indicates that it is in the nature of inspiration itself to be incomplete, enigmatic, vague: "La mercancía que suministra la inspiración acostumbra a ser breve, circunstancial y en muchos casos incompleta. Su extensión se limita a unas pocas palabras y, a lo sumo, a ciertas insinuaciones que en cuanto materia prima que el

escritor debe elaborar, analizar y formalizar, se presentan más
como problemas que como soluciones" (p. 45). Clearly, these ideas
are descriptive of the effects, for the general reader, of Benet's own
writing.

Despite the frequent appearance of the concepts of indefiniteness,
incompleteness, mystery, and plurisignation, Benet does not advocate ambiguity, as opposed to clarity, on the basis of its natural
inherence in language as a medium. Perhaps this is so because
"natural" or characteristic multiple meanings interest him less than
artistically created polyvalence. He terms willful vagueness or indefiniteness "muy apta para la invención y la ficción" (p. 51), and
further states:

La indeterminación es una adopción disimulada que sólo cobra su verdadero alcance cuando el narrador se decide a remodelar y rellenar . . . de
acuerdo con sus deseos, con sus situaciones, sus personajes y sus histo-
rietas. Por eso, y viceversa, cuando al narrador le conviene de entrada
poner de manifiesto el carácter ficticio de su relato lo primero que hace es
echar mano a una indeterminación específica. (p. 51)

Ambiguity, the *bête noir* of a host of classical rhetoricians, was
intellectually rehabilitated in the present century by William Emp-
son (*The Seven Types of Ambiguity*, 1931). Benet does not use this
term so much as a variety of synonyms, but ambiguity is the most
accurate word to describe the result of many of these fictional and
stylistic practices.

If inspiration is obscure and paradoxical, Benet argues that neither is style rational, as indicated by the incapability of reason to
invent an instrument with which to measure, define, or analyze it.
That ambiguous or irrational quality, as opposed to clarity and
logic, is viewed as positive. Citations from Read, which Benet appropriates and elaborates, are especially suggestive: "El lenguaje del
poeta es esencial y normalmente oscuro, dice Herbert Read (*The
Nature of Literature*), pero esa oscuridad no es tanto una nota
negativa del poeta sino del lector, quien en su lenguaje, es claro y
lógico a costa de ser inexacto y superficial . . . (El poema) dice
Read, es impermeable a la razón y *si carece de un significado preciso su poder es inmenso*" (p. 158; italics mine). Ambiguity, the opposite of clarity and precision, is thus implicitly defended by Benet

as less "inexacto y superficial" than what is conveyed by clear and logical language.

Objectivity and precision are viewed as antagonistic to what Benet understands inspiration to be:

Creo recordar que fue Flaubert quien afirmó que no conocía ningún género de inspiración capaz de resistir diez horas de trabajo de corrección. No hay duda de que la inspiración tiene poco o nada que ver con aquella objetividad y aquella precisión por las que tanto se afanó . . . Pero él no debió solicitarla (inspiración) nunca, y tal vez por eso no se distinguió jamás ni por su riqueza de metáforas ni por la brillantez de su vocabulario. (p. 84)

Mystery and the indefinable, however, receive high marks from Benet, and he devotes an entire essay to the legendary ghost ships such as the "Flying Dutchman" ("Algo acerca del buque fantasma"). Benet relates this specifically to the narrative: "La invención del misterio (en la novela de ese nombre o en cualquier otro género, clásico o moderno, de análoga configuración) cumple un doble objeto al poner de manifiesto *el interés que despierta todo enigma*" (p. 144; italics mine). The author's thinking here is clearly applicable to his own fictional inventions. He lauds what he terms the *novela del mar* likewise for possessing "una suerte de misterio permanente, de vagos y sutiles contornos" (p. 145). Turning to Poe, he observes, "el misterio prevalece, es un fin en sí mismo que no puede ni debe ser resuelto y que cobra todo su valor por su carácter absurdo, fantástico y fatídico" (p. 145), an apt description of many cryptic episodes in Benet's own work. The legend of the ghost ship merits Benet's praise for the reason that its mystery, insoluble by definition, will continue ipso facto to exercise an endless fascination.

Like the mysterious, the strange or marvelous holds an attraction; in the absence of these, style must compensate: "el escritor se convencerá pronto de que, en cuanto logre hacer interesante lo banal, lo cotidiano y lo antihistórico, contará con un artificio válido por sí mismo que sabe prescindir, sin pignorar su atractivo, de las facilidades que ofrece la historia" (p. 168). This too has a large area of applicability to the fictions of Benet. He does not advocate, however, the recounting of daily events for their own sake: "Creo recordar que Joyce escribió algo parecido; algo así como que el nove-

lista debe hablar de lo ordinario, pues lo extraordinario queda para
el periodista. Parece la profesión de fe de un costumbrista; si ese
precepto se convirtiera en ley de orden público habría que retirar de
las librerías las mejores novelas que ha escrito el hombre" (p. 169).
Here again, Benet is at odds with classical rhetorical principles,
with their emphasis on fact, reason, and example.

   While Benet carefully points out that he is not attempting to construct an irrationalist theory of literary style (p. 161), he makes
clear that the communication of specific content or meaning is less
to be desired than the creation of "una unidad de orden superior a
la mera representación de un significado concreto" (p. 163). Benet's
narratives as a whole are seldom reducible to "la mera representación de un significado concreto," from which it may be deduced
that he employs, at least to some extent, a consciously elaborated
rhetoric (or antirhetoric) of his own in deliberate avoidance of univocal clarity, logic, precision, and specificity. Content, meaning, or
message are not primary concerns, but subordinate to a mysterious
or unexplained "unidad de orden superior." Although probably
more viable as a theory of art than of communication, it does suf-
fice to establish Benet's position vis-à-vis the mainstream of contemporary rhetorical theory. In sum, Benet as rhetorician is anticlassical, as artist antirealist or antimimetic. Rhetorically, he is
opposed not only to suasion, but to the communication of doctrine
or ideological content. "Message" is subordinate to the medium.
Benet's formulations constitute a sort of counterrhetoric or meta-
rhetoric (for he is not antirhetorical in the usual connotation of
that term).

   Rhetoricians ancient and modern have, despite differences among
themselves, been near unanimity in their agreement upon certain
key principles: clarity, logic, the presentation of facts or ideas with
reasonable economy and speed, or without unnecessary verbosity.
The traditional view of rhetoric as persuasion has yielded in this
century, at least in part, to the emphasis upon communication, with
a simultaneous broadening of the discipline to encompass media
other than speech or the written word, and embracing arts other
than the literary or forensic. Philosopher-rhetorician Kenneth Burke,
for example, holds that art is a means of communication and as

such is certainly designed to elicit a response of some sort. Thus, he reasons that "under conditions of competitive capitalism, there must necessarily be a large corrective or propaganda element in art." Burke's notion of art, and subsequently of rhetoric, falls within the classical tradition, insofar as he posits a "hortatory function, an element of suasion or inducement."[2] For this theorist, the basic function of rhetoric is the "use of words by human agents to form attitudes or to induce actions in other human agents."[3]

Earlier in the century, Ivor A. Richards envisioned the proper sphere of rhetorical inquiry as the study of misunderstanding and its remedies, an analysis of verbal understanding and misunderstanding. Reacting against the emphasis on debate or disputation, he contended that exposition is also a rhetorical aim. While very modern in considering all language and thought as essentially metaphorical,[4] Richards's position is less anticlassical than a particular subdivision of classicism, for he appropriates the principle of adaptation of discourse to its ends, and continues to stress clarity: "How to make minds clear as well as keep them clear is . . . for us, as it was for Socrates, the key question."[5]

Central to much contemporary rhetorical debate is the relationship between rhetoric and communication, a relationship that varies in accord with differing views of communication as dialogue or as polemic. Despite the fact that rhetoric has suffered some loss of respectability in modern times because of association with the persuasion/manipulation/exploitation syndrome, and despite rejection by some theorists of the debating function (which Richards disparagingly termed a "puppy war with words"), a number of contemporary theoreticians have defended and refurbished the function of disputation. Chaim Perelman in *The New Rhetoric* (1969) stresses practical argumentation, drawing largely upon classical and Renaissance sources.[6] Consciously audience-oriented, his two-volume study examines the structure of verbal argument, oral and written, with attention to classical canons of style and organization. His analysis first centers on the types of proofs discussed by Aristotle, with reference to Plato, Quintilian, Cicero, and other classical sources, and Pascal and Bossuet among the moderns. Subsequently, Perelman explores the framework of argumentation and attempts to construct a model of practical argument, drawn primarily from jurisprudence. Similarly, Stephen Toulmin draws on forensic procedures in an effort to develop and elaborate a real-life logic of argumentation.[7]

Benet is clearly as far removed from these contemporary rhetoricians as he is from the *Rhetorica ad Herenium* and the classical notions of narrative proceeding from the brief, lucid, and plausible exposition of fact. Indeed, among today's numerous exponents of rhetoric and communications theory, the one to whom Benet is closest is Marshall McLuhan. This is not to suggest that Benet is a McLuhanite, for even the most superficial comparison will reveal sweeping divergences, but rather to call attention to their coincidence on certain fundamental principles.

McLuhan argues that during the ages of the phonetic alphabet and the printing press, perception became visual, linear, and sequential. He saw each new communications medium as altering "ratios" of sense perception in those exposed. Media in the present electronic age combine the early (tribal) oral mode and "mosaic" perception, and have changed our views of reality and rationality, imperiling the linear and sequential pattern of thought.[8] As David Hume showed in the eighteenth century, there is no necessary principle of causality in a mere sequence; that one thing follows another accounts for nothing. It is abundantly clear in Benet's fiction that nothing follows from following except change, which supposedly would reflect the "mosaic" or nonlinear and nonsequential perception. McLuhan contends that the greatest of all reversals occurred with electricity, which ended sequence by making things instant. Similarly, the movie, in his view, by sheer speeding up of the mechanical, carried us from the world of sequence and connections into a world of creative configuration and structure. The "message" of the movie medium is therefore deemed to be one of transition from lineal connectedness to configuration.

Rational, says McLuhan, has for the West long meant "uniform, continuous and sequential." Western man has confused reason, literacy, and rationalism with a single technology (a reference to printing). Thus in the electric age man seems to the conventional West to become irrational. McLuhan is concerned with the effects of technology on psychic formation, and the demand of technology that we behave in uniform and continuous patterns. In proclaiming that "the medium is the message," McLuhan sees "message" as equatable with the impact on human sensory perception patterns and on institutions. For him, the medium, more than the *content* of communication, carries the societally significant message. Thus, he believes that the medium of print has done more to revolutionize society than the content of the printed words, just as the alphabet, the telegraph, television, and other media have reshaped basic messages, reorienting their very content. McLuhan's focus, of course, is the medium rather than the message, and his work raises fundamental questions about the importance of content in the rhetorical process.

Benet approximates the stance of McLuhan in his insistence upon a given medium (style) at the expense of message. When Benet advocates the creation of "una unidad de orden superior a la mera representación de un significado concreto" and speaks against the transmission of opinions and doctrines, he is relegating content of message to a subordinate position, quite consistent with his downgrading of logic, clarity, and precision. Neither really discusses message, but both are concerned with ways in which the medium controls the amount and the configuration of information, of ideas, of communication itself. Contemporary rhetoricians generally have moved away from the emphasis upon persuasion, preferring the concept of communication, but to most this implies something to be communicated—a message. McLuhan focuses not upon the end result of communication (reception of a message) so much as the process of transmisson, particularly by the electronic media. Benet is concerned only with the written word, but like McLuhan, he deemphasizes content. Exposition is not an end in itself, nor is suasion, the formation of attitudes, or even understanding. What Benet seeks as the end product of his rhetoric is enigma, insolubility, ambiguity.

Neither McLuhan nor Benet discusses "traditional" rhetoric (there is no allusion to the more or less standard catalog of figures and devices), but both display an impressive command of the standard tools. Benet is, of course, far less ambitious, and less frequently guilty of overgeneralization, of begging the question, and logical inconsistencies. His preoccupation is aesthetic, while McLuhan's is not, and questions of influence are most improbable. While many of Benet's principles seem almost a parodic inversion of classical rhetorical precepts, it is clear that, as with Cervantes and the *Quijote*, the result greatly transcends mere parody. Benet's rhetoric of noncommunication, plurisignation, non-suasion, obscurity and imprecision, his subordination of concrete meaning and his exaltation of style as an artifice capable of endowing the most banal subjects with interest—all are exemplified in his fiction, which constitutes an impressive display of virtuosity in the adaptation of traditional figures and devices to the purposes of rhetoric of ambiguity.

ESTHER W. NELSON

# Narrative Perspective in
# "Volverás a Región"

The past disposes its heavy folds
around thought, forming layer
after layer of confused
remembrances.

GEORGES POULET[1]

It is certain, the reader who sets out to assemble a coherent perception of the fictional world in *Volverás a Región* is obligated to do so
by wending his way through a verbal maze created by multiple perspectives: that of an undramatized third-person narrator; of Daniel
Sebastián, a doctor who lives in seclusion, caring only for a single
patient, a retarded and emotionally disturbed man; of Marré Gamallo, a woman close to fifty, daughter of a Falangist general killed
during the Spanish Civil War who has come to see Sebastián in an
effort to locate his godson, Luis I. Timoner, a Republican captain
who had been her lover during the war and who, during its final
days, fled into the mountains where he had been raised. Although
there is a sense of a world in linear time, we cannot totally ap-
prehend the sequence of events because they are presented in juxtaposition by narrative voices whose perspective is synoptic: all
events are seen to exist simultaneously in consciousness, coming
into focus in the persistently repetitive manner of memory, which
records events spatially and in their relationships to other events,
and not in their temporal context and duration.[2]

The perspective of the undramatized narrator is subjective and
obsessive, communicating by his tone an alienation from the reality

28                                          ESTHER W. NELSON

he projects. We can only guess at the degree of his distortion, since other facets of the narrative are presented by equally autistic narrators. What emerges is a phantasmagoric world isolated in an atmosphere of ruin, as difficult to enter as to leave, where even physical laws are unreliable: "el viajero que . . . pretende llegar a su sierra . . . . Un momento u otro conocerá el desaliento al sentir que cada paso hacia adelante no hace sino alejarlo un poco más de aquellas desconocidas montañas" (p. 7).[3] Immediately we are reminded of Kafka's *Castle*, in which the distance between K and the castle increases as he proceeds toward it. Likewise in *Volverás a Región*, time flow is paralyzed, displaced in part by a mythical time sense conferred by such figures as the *barquera* and the legendary Numa; even the air seems to stagnate. There is never an image of freshness or newness to relieve the monotony of the malignant terrain, which is seen as a willful and menacing entity. Repeated images of decay combine with a sense of fatalism to convey a unity of nightmare to the fictional world. And the initial suggestion that "tal vez la decadencia empieza una manaña de las postrímerias del verano" (p. ll) is later reversed; the notion of there ever having been a glorious and honorable past is a delusion (pp. 14, 47).

At times there is a distinctly oneiric quality to the reality transmitted by the narrator: "aquellos hombres y mujeres fosforescentes que . . . solían en el verano concentrarse en un caserón de las riberas altas del Torce" (p. 216). Our suspicion of his epistemological position is reinforced by his acceptance of phenomena that can only be classed as supernatural occurrences—a mysterious red glow in the Mantuan forest, the traveler's painful sensation of being stung in the back while attempting to make his way to Región, the disembodied sounds of motor vehicles, a strange bird of prey—even when he occasionally attributes them to hearsay. His vision operates as a filter that excludes anything beautiful or positive. When his focus narrows, his intensity is magnified, and the fictional world and its inhabitants are subjected to increased scrutiny: the landscape, at other times viewed synchronically in its historical verticality as a battleground since ancient times, is now described in its particular configurations, as by one who is himself lost in the brambles. But it becomes paradoxically more indistinct in proportion to the precision with which it is depicted, and the predominance of disquieting imagery confirms our supposition that rather than the surrounding geography the narrator is describing its effects on his spirit.[4]

In contrast to the oppressive density of the geographical descriptions, the situation appears vague. In the opening line of the novel, the play on the word "real" alerts the reader to the ambiguity he will encounter with regard to reality: "Es cierto, el viajero que saliendo de Región pretende llegar a su sierra siguiendo el antiguo camino real—porque el moderno dejó de serlo—se ve obligado a atravesar un pequeño y elevado desierto que parece interminable" (p. 7). Ricardo Gullón has observed that from the first, the narrator seems to be addressing someone who has asked him a question.[5] But to whom does he speak? There is no response from anyone within the work; and yet the language presumes an audience whose knowledge is intimately associated and perhaps identical with that of the speaker. At times he assumes an omniscient perspective; at others he appears ignorant, forgetful, confused, or apathetic, as though he had said or at least thought it all before (pp. 101, 216, 259, 271). At first he does not seem to know what Marré has taken from her purse: "¿era tal vez una fotografía?" (p. 101), but later he remembers: "En el borde de la mesa estaba aún la fotografía. No era una tarjeta" (p. 312), as though the person he were addressing were not the reader who had already been given that information by the doctor: "mientras quede una postal, una fotografía amarillenta como ésa que usted trae " (p. 253). He seems, in fact, to be engaging in an interior monologue that oscillates between conscious and subconscious levels and is directed only incidentally at himself.

The narrator also acts as a center of consciousness for other characters. The world, as seen by the idiot, comprises a limited sphere of simple images obscured by solitude and incomprehension: a bleakly furnished house, the old Adela cooking and sewing, a bone-colored table, the taste of unseasoned rice, a gold brooch, a black car that took his mother away. The past, as vivid in his conciousness as the present, is brought into the foreground and narrated as dramatic scene.

Daniel Sebastián and Marré Gamallo appear as multilayered composites of their experiences, bearing the indelible mark of their entire cultural context and of the persons and events that have touched their lives. Their accounts appear within the work as un-commented recollection, as other visions of the events, and of the fictional universe. The reader is allowed to probe their conscious-ness and thereby capture their loneliness, confusion, and despair.

Reality, in Daniel's view, is altered by his fatalistic conception of time as "la dimensión en que la persona humana sólo puede ser des-graciada" (p. 257) and by his fear of progress, symbolized by a *rueda* that his father used as an oracle, combining mystical occultism with technology. Progress, he believes, has caused irreversible changes in reality that are accepted as inherent (p. 217) and has unleashed evil by eliminating the concrete and relatively minor fears that once dis-tracted our ancestors from the deeper, existential terror we now en-dure. In addition, progress is responsible for the diminished status of the individual (p. 222). Acting together, progress and time pro-duce a sense of *miedo* without an object (p. 222). Intellectually Daniel recognizes that Numa may exist only as a subjective, albeit collective, projection: "Quizá ya no existe sino como cristalización del temor o como la fórmula que describe (y justifica) la composi-ción del residuo de un cuerpo del que se sublimaron todos los de-seos" (p. 221). At no time, however, does he (or the narrator) dis-play a scientific curiosity or determination to verify or dispel this and the many other unexplained phenomena. Anguish is relieved only by his occasional bitter sarcasm and bizarre observations about reality or by viewing it dispassionately as a stage (pp. 223–25). Daniel attempts to free himself from historical time and the cause-and-effect relationships of an external world in decay by im-prisoning himself in a subjective, almost solipsistic present, where his only activity consists of compulsive self-contemplation. Yet his internal conquest of time is only partial: images of the past per-sistently intrude into his thoughts.

Marré's view of reality is far less pessimistic, uncolored by Daniel's obsession with the destructiveness of time. According to her view, the future is cast in a somewhat positive light because of the quest she has undertaken, and the past is consecrated by the memory of the love she shared with Luis and which she continually seeks to reexperience in thought. Daniel's indifference to the past and lack of faith in the future is underscored when he attempts to dissuade her from her mission (p. 103). Marré's greater objectivity enables her to recognize that the differences in their appraisal of the same reality are the result of perspective relativity: "Usted no me ve con fuerzas para continuar el viaje y yo no me veo con salud para abandonarlo; una vez más porque presenciamos la misma circunstancia desde dos puntos de vista algo diferentes" (p. 264). Her objectivity also enables her to distinguish three distinct aspects of her own personality (pp. 149–53) and to acknowledge the prismatic power of memory clouded by psychological distance (p. 301).

Another perspective is that of one who we may call the "editor," whose view of the events appears in footnotes, and who, because his account of Daniel's marriage (pp. 275–77) contradicts those of the narrator (pp. lll, 257), may be assumed to be another voice (although with no certainty, since the narrator contradicts himself). The final perspective is that of another agent, the implied author who, with little compassion for the reader, creates and presents the verbal constructs: the exterior space of Región, its environs, legends, and inhabitants, and the events that appear as images of the inner world.[6]

The fragmented structure of the novel reflects the instability of the fictional world as viewed by the several narrating voices. Images from the past recur in confused sequence in a monotonous rhythm to dominate the present; long descriptions paralyze the flow of time in the exterior chronology, which encompasses a duration of a few hours, from one evening to the following morning. The chaotic and incomplete presentation of events reflects the predominance of intuitive over rational thought processes. This is not a novel of spatial presentation whose fragments can eventually be reordered and apprehended as a complete and coherent image.[7] Here the story line is also presented as lengths of broken thread, but the reader, encouraged by a few clues to hope others will emerge, will retain many cross-referents of images in vain. Extensive use is made of ellipsis, and any attempt to connect the fragments leads to contradiction and paradox; the reader cannot furnish to the text what is not there. Efforts to arrange the events according to clock and calendar time are as futile as trying to reweave a piece of fabric that was full of holes before being unraveled. The omission of key events conveys the disregard for external reality of a consciousness that has withdrawn into itself, in this instance applicable to the undramatized narrator as well as the two characters. The importance of the events is not related to their place in historical time but to their prominence in the inner world.

The exterior events presented by the narrator are limited to the exchange of a few words by Daniel and Marré, the murder of the former by his demented patient/ward, and the implied death of Marré at the hands of Numa. However, we do not observe Marré's departure. (When the narrator says there was a shot the following morning, can we believe him? Does he belong to the fictional fabric as much as the characters? Is he not just as drugged by the hallucinogenic reality he portrays as any of them?) Parts of conversations are obviously omitted and external silences are interrupted by words that do not follow in meaning. In the beginning, for example, we watch with Daniel as he first sees Marré through a window and hear him say to himself, "Ha llegado usted, aunque algo tarde" (p. 99), as though he has been waiting for her; but when she starts to introduce herself, "Mi nombre es . . .," he cuts her off, not by saying "Ya lo sé," or "la reconozco," but with the strangely inappropriate words, "Oh, no hablemos de eso" (p. 113). Later, when recounting (to himself? aloud?) incidents of his family background, he suddenly asks, "¿Me decía usted algo? Creía . . .," and immediately, in the next paragraph, adds, "Tonterías. Lleva usted muy poco tiempo aquí para haberse vuelto tan supersticiosa. Tonterías, acomodaciones de la imaginación," and goes on with his tale, "No le diré cómo fueron mis años de estudiante" (p. 130). And when Marré pauses, as she relates an event of the past, Daniel remarks, "Tenemos un solo árbol . . . pero ¿ha visto usted cómo brilla?" and the woman continues, " . . . no en la guerra sino en la paz" (p. 158). The simplicity of their words when they explicitly address one another contrasts with the baroque circumlocutions of the interior monologues, where the recurrence of synecdoche and pronouns with ambiguous antecedents indicate that in general Daniel and

Marré are mentally reviewing events and reliving sensations, so precise identification is unnecessary. The reader, however, cannot always distinguish between their thoughts and the words they articulate or how much each hears of what the other says. There is little in the way of conversation and nothing at all of real communication. The motif of submergence occurs in a social sense: they share nothing but their location in space and in sequential time; each is totally isolated and the only contact between them is superficial. Their perception of time is obscured by their morbid indulgence in daydream, where emotional, biological, and cultural aspects of existence predominate, renewing feelings of defeat and remorse, while reason seems only to turn back on itself and run into dead ends.

The literary space is expanded through the technique of narrative stasis in the exposition of "present" events and again within the interior monologues, as thoughts drift to other recollections that in turn are interrupted by further digressions into earlier or later periods. The interior chronology spans a period from the childhood of Gamallo and Sebastián to the present moment, the 1960s, focusing on certain events in the decades of the 1910s and 1920s and especially of the period of the Civil War, but bypassing almost entirely those of the intervening postwar years. The occasional instances of summary, such as the long footnote and the accounts of Daniel's marriage, are sketchy and incomplete. Continuity is destroyed by abrupt shifts in the narrative perspective or in the object of attention: unexpectedly we find ourselves observing another location, another time frame. Through the various narrative voices we receive fragmentary descriptions, superimposed images, details diffused or enhanced by memory, vagueness with regard to time locus, motifs that confuse rather than clarify the situation. *Morosidad*, a quality praised by Ortega y Gasset, becomes excruciating, for by the time we are presented with another fragment of story line, we may have had to read a hundred pages of divagations and even then be met only with disconnected images that invalidate our previous conceptions of the situation. Not only the fable, but the entire fictional universe appears distant and difficult to grasp, even though linguistic signification is maintained throughout, for the narrators are describing a reality with which they are so intimate that the seemingly endless parenthetical intrusions, the repetitive negative phrasing, and the excessive adjectivization are of no consequence: they are not addressing us.

The narration is forwarded by the principles of metonymic digression, as though it were dealing with a referent external to itself, implicitly an area of Spain during the twentieth century. Symbols are taken from experience and related casually to their meaning instead of embodying the essence of a purely internal referent. The narrative follows a path of contiguous relationship from plot to interior imagery to descriptions of the landscape, to views of characters identified partially ("la mano agarrotada," "la sortija," "gruesos cristales," "gabán de color tabaco," "el velo," "él") or not at all. Although the entire fictional world is an interior one, the techniques of surrealism are largely absent in the general context of the novel. Occasional instances of cynical or macabre humor and grotesque images, such as the descriptions of the *barquera* and of Daniel's mother, appear amidst the pervasive atmosphere of ruin, mystery, and despair.

All the narrative perspectives focus on existential concerns: the yearning for communion, continuity of life and of the self, seen in such motifs as geographic and human barrenness; eternal activity of an immanent nature; the inexorability of death and decay, reflected in the pejorative progression of events in the plot; the abandoning or destructive parent; and on social themes only in their universal significance: the repression of the individual by social institutions, the *derkou theama* of classical tragedy (Adela/Muerte/suegra, as well as the *rueda*), and war. But no partisan case is made for either faction: we are shown the psychological and spiritual destruction wrought upon persons on both sides of the conflict: victors and vanquished, leaders and those in the lowest echelons. It is uncertain whether man himself or some fate is responsible for his plight, and the individual is powerless to do anything about it: "Todo . . . ha venido a parar en que ya nadie explota pero todos somos explotados, por el estado, por la religión, por el bien común, por lo que sea y contra lo que nadie puede luchar de forma que lejos de suprimir la explotación lo que se ha hecho es transformarla en cosa invulnerable y sacramental" (p. 222).

There is no sense of harmony with a cosmic order in the novel. Numa's restoration of "el silencio habitual del lugar" (p. 315) is not related to the classical nemesis, but serves only to fulfill in some measure the desire for stability and order, however negative or repressive, of "un pueblo cobarde, egoísta y soez [que] prefiere siempre la represión a la incertidumbre" (p. 222), symbolized by the group that gathers at the tower of the church of El Salvador to listen for the inevitable carbine shot after any vehicle is seen driving toward the sierra. The characters appear to have as little control of themselves as of their circumstances: they lack the zeal and enterprise either to survive or to do away with themselves. The degree of guilt, despair, self-hatred, and revulsion they assume seems pathological, while their anguish transcends what we feel would have normally been produced in a healthy person by an absent or oppressive parent, or by having been rejected by a lover. The subjective impressions about the childhood of Daniel and that of Gamallo and of his daughter appear as phenomenological descriptions. The psychology of the characters is not analyzed by the narrator, and we are precluded from judging the normalcy of their psychological adjustment. The underlying cause of their suffering is obviously spiritual rather than emotional: it is the solitude of the individual who cannot find inner peace and is alienated from his context.

The style in which Daniel's thoughts are given is occasionally so indistinguishable from that of the narrator in his description of the landscape, in the weariness of his tone, the continued use of "es cierto," and his references to himself in the third person that the reader is compelled to retrace his steps to see where he may have missed a closing of quotation marks. The marks do eventually appear, but much later. On several occasions, Daniel becomes quite as "omniscient" as the undramatized narrator, recounting events at which he was not present, such as the dialogues between the miners (pp. 203–5), and transmitting the thoughts of the gambler, whom he apparently knew only by sight at the casino half a century earlier (p. 207). Puzzled by his ability to adopt an omniscient pose to relate this and the incident of the shepherdess (pp. 224–25), we check again to assure ourselves that what we are experiencing is not the view of the narrator. But then a few lines later, Daniel once again addresses his visitor ("Y a este respecto quiero una vez más llamarle la atención. . ." [p. 225]) and continues his discourse. His identity as narrator is also in doubt when he gives his view of the incident at the gaming table, for although he is presumably speaking to Marré, he refers to Gamallo always as "aquel militar," "el presunto amante de María Timoner," or "el joven teniente," never as "su padre"; and the doubt increases when, although the quotation marks which opened his words (p. 216) have not closed and first-person references have frequently appeared, Daniel is suddenly mentioned in the third person: "Al poco rato [el minero] había perdido todas sus ganancias que habían pasado a manos del militar; ya estaban solos, en el salón vecino—casi todas las luces apagadas—sólo quedaba su prometida con aquel joven doctor que seguía su tratamiento en la clínica de Sardú y que constituía su escolta todas las noches de juego . . . y . . . se levantó de la silla: 'María, Daniel, venid aquí que esto merece verse,' dijo" (p. 231); and later, "no había enfrente más que la sortija, y detrás de ellos, María; y detrás de María, el joven e inexperto doctor" (p. 233). The undramatized narrator takes over, at this point, to recount some of the events that led up to the wager and of Daniel's hope of winning María for himself, and continues the motif of reality-as-stage begun by Daniel (p. 244), who in turn takes up the same perspective as the narrator, but bringing the events of the past into present tense (p. 245).

At times reality appears grotesque under Daniel's intensive gaze: "Todos los cuerpos se rebulleron en las literas como los gusanos, al levantar una piedra" (p. 204); at other times the doctor seems spiritually dead, devoid of sentiments about anything in the present. A constant barrage of sensory and informative images reflects his inability to calibrate reality in any logical order or to cope with "el así llamado progreso," an inability he considers an instinctive survival mechanism: "Sin duda existe en nuestro cuerpo una cierta válvula defensiva gracias a la cual la razón se niega a aceptar lo irremediable, lo caducable; porque debe ser muy difícil existir si se pierde la convicción de que mientras dure la vida sus posibilidades son inagotables y casi infinitas" (p. 127).

In contrast to Daniel's wish to evade images of what has gone before and any thought of the future, Marré allows her thoughts to wander into the past, to savor erotic recollections that are inter-woven with painful memories. Through her the reader receives al-most no view of the landscape or its legends, for her perspective is directed inward. External objects in her narration appear in relation to events—the mud into which Gerd's body fell, a fence associated with a young soldier killed during the war, the truck and the inn where her first sexual experiences occurred. The excessive use of long contrived analogies reflects the intensity of her preoccupation with her unfulfilled yearnings. The sexual desires of a young girl ed-ucated in a convent are phrased in images reminiscent of Renais-sance surrealism: "el chisporroteo lujuriante de partículas incan-descentes (vapores viciados por el anhelo, esperanzas sumergidas en la pasión, ideales retraídos por el apetito) . . . tejidos desgarrados al rojo por la llama masculina . . . fragmentos irrecomponibles" (p. 295). Marré's search does not represent a wish to recapture the past in an effort to escape the present, but to redeem the past by finding Luis, the only person who can open the way for her to live with integrity in the present. For since her "wanton" behavior dur-ing the war, which had followed upon a restrictive upbringing, she has married and rigidly observed the appearances demanded by so-ciety, thus repressing her authentic self.

In summary, the fictional universe of *Volverás a Región* is de-picted by Daniel Sebastián, Marré Gamallo, a third-person narra-tor, and the author of the footnotes to the text, which follow the same obscure manner of expression as that of the other voices.[8] There is no empirical view of the external reality of Región; it is not presented within a neutral context that would allow the reader to gauge the degree to which it is being disfigured by the untrustwor-thy narrator and the characters who transmit it to us. We hope in vain for objective guideposts within the linguistic tangle, for a source from which we might glean the material we need to judge the accuracy of what lies before us. Instead, a sense of layering is produced by the multiplicity of perspectives: that of the implied au-thor who presents the entire verbal space and presumably knows the "truth," that of the enigmatic "editor," that of the undrama-tized narrator, those of Marré and Daniel, and finally those of the voices who speak within the memories of the latter, such as Luis

Timoner (pp. 109–11), the doctor's parents-in-law, the miners, and the many anonymous subjects of "dicen que" and "se dice." The reader is in the presence of a world resembling those elaborate Chinese ivory carvings whose concentric spheres can never be perceived simultaneously or in their entirety, but only segmentally, by aligning apertures in the adjacent spheres, and whose innermost layers seem to continue to infinity.

NELSON R. ORRINGER

# Epic in a Paralytic State: "Volverás a Región"

*In memory of my father*

The epic does not always show the hero advancing straightaway toward the fulfillment of his destiny. Sometimes weak-willed moments set in. In the *Iliad*, perhaps the best-known of all Western epics, Achilles, governed by wrath and pride, lingers through much of the poem at the side of the battlefield instead of undertaking his mission to defeat the Trojans. In the *Odyssey*, Ulysses tarries for years in returning to the home and throne that belong to him by right. He spends that time threatened by the dangers and wooed by the charms of the sea. Indeed, Ortega y Gasset has called him "el primer Don Juan." When he flees his workaday Penelope, he finds all the charming creatures of our sea, wins their love, and flees them.[1] Ulysses has an imitator in the hero of the *Aeneas*: pursued by an angry Juno on his way to founding the city of Rome, he must surmount many obstacles, among them, the love of Dido. The temptation of heroes even passes into the Christian epic. Dante's dialogues with spirits in Hell and with souls in Purgatory detain him from rising at once to salvation.

But let us recall an episode from the *Odyssey*, whose heavy influence on the modern novel may stem from the suspense produced by mounting tension when heroism undergoes paralysis.[2] At the start of Book II, Antinous, one of Penelope's suitors, confesses to her son Telemachus that she has deceived them for five years: during that time, she has promised to choose a new husband as soon as she completed weaving the shroud for the father of the missing Ulysses;

yet she has unraveled by night and in secret what she has woven by day.

An epic could be written whose narrator's irony matched that of the deceived Antinous. That narrator could also display Penelope's skill in destroying each figure and action he presented. The hero of this epic might, like Ulysses, remain away from his house in ruins and his unprotected people. The description of such a work in fact fits *Volverás a Región*, the 1967 novel that critics have regarded as an epic without applying this concept to it in any rigorous sense. José Ortega has written that in Región the thwarted epic of the Civil War suits the play of appearances and illusions; in short, what has most to do with the passing of time. The epic genre is the most flexible of all in bearing witness to time. It evokes a mixture of the three times: past, present, and future.[3] History invites prophecy, much the way a hero asks a wise old shade in the underworld to reveal his future to him. In the classical epic, however, the hero usually fulfills his destiny, whether or not it is foretold to him. Achilles at last attacks the Trojans, and Ulysses wreaks his vengeance on Penelope's suitors. In *Volverás a Región*, a novel cut of Penelope's cloth, the skein of passing time always seems to come unraveled. Ortega rightfully describes Región as a space in which time has ceased to move.[4] To show that the novel is a paralyzed epic, I shall first summarize Benet's ideas on epic as set down in his essays. Next I shall point out the effect of the epic on the structure of his novel of 1967. Then, Benet's epic or mock-epic depiction of nature in Región, its hero, and its civil war will be examined. Finally, the epic will be related to the points of view of three main characters, Dr. Daniel Sebastián, Colonel Gamallo's daughter, and the demented war orphan.

In his essays, Benet defines epic as "una clase de poesía alta y exclusivamente especializada en narrar unos hechos . . . que, cualquiera que sea su naturaleza, todos tienen una circunstancia en común: el ojo humano no los ha visto nunca; para comprenderlos no se puede echar mano a la experiencia del hombre con sus semejantes y su naturaleza."[5] When the poet presents a likeness between the epic world and quotidian reality, he simply renders daily events with "otras dimensiones" (p. 20). To depict conflicts between gods, for instance, he need only describe human wars, but "on another scale." If he is to be understood, he must "dejar bien clara la proporcionalidad entre ambas series de imágenes" (p. 22). Still, the epic style, like every human invention, cannot escape the corrosive action of time. In the essay "La entrada en la taberna," published in 1966 (the year before *Volverás a Región*), Benet singles out for study a special moment in the development of styles, the point when they have passed their prime and seek renewal by approaching popular tastes, even by adopting colloquial expressions on occasion. To employ Benet's figured language, "En tal momento la epopeya, cansada tal vez de tanto héroe y tanto Olimpo, entra furtivamente en la taberna para descansar sus dilatadas pupilas con las medias luces de los interiores humildes."[6] But Benet suggests that any deviation from the lofty style, if it serves no critical or iconoclastic purpose, is lacking in sincerity.

Since the sixteenth century, according to Benet, Spanish art has almost always reflected a taste for what is popular and homespun. In many works of the Golden Age (1550–1650), this taste is blended with a subtle critique of the state. Between the lines is found a charge of statism, leveled at a political order that one day took it upon itself to "despertar la conciencia del país y apoderarse de ella para sus propios fines y que—lo hemos venido a comprobar palmariamente en el siglo XX—el pueblo tiene que aceptar sin rechistar" (p. 80). But the Spanish people, as viewed by Benet, have no imperial aspirations, no cosmopolitan breadth of focus, no true faith in the collective programs forced upon them from above. Hence a work like *Don Quixote* may well be "una parábola de las vicisitudes de un Estado delirante que para llevar a cabo su insensata función redentora necesita seducir. . .a un plebeyo remolón para que le acompañe y asista, pero que a la postre termina por conducirle a la vieja humilde casona, para concluir en paz sus días, rodeado de ruinas, una vez pasado el soplo de locura" (p. 81). Accordingly, the epic style of *Don Quixote* loses in eloquence, enthusiasm, and energy what it gains in irony, skepticism, and resignation. In sum, "la épica, como una pecadora arrepentida, decidió vestirse con la arpillera de la prosa y mudarse hacia la novela para cantar las gracias—ya que no las glorias—de las ventas castellanas" (p. 87). If, therefore, Cervantes's epic shows disillusionment with the oppressive Spanish state of the sixteenth century, it would probably not force Benet's text to see *Volverás a Región* as a similar epic vis-à-vis twentieth-century Spanish statism, whether of a liberal or a conservative ideology.

The organization of Benet's novel would seem to indicate as much. The first of the four parts into which he divides the work depicts an untamed nature, whose strength attains mythical proportions, reducing man to impotence. Benet describes in slow motion the Civil War of Región and in this fashion gives the conflict a mock-epic cast. In the second part, two alienated characters, Dr. Sebastián and Gamallo's daughter, soliloquize at length after the war about their loss of faith in Spanish national history. The physician reveals in the third part, as Gamallo's daughter does in the fourth, the personal motives behind each one's disillusionment. In both cases, the thwarting of heroism plays a main role in depriving the character of hope.

The forbidding landscape of Región makes its presence felt on every page. The land belongs to the world of the epic, for the human eye has never seen or known its reality, its mysterious essence. Hence Benet treats with an ironic barb an imagined tourist passing through this imaginary terrain. Here we have the traveler who plods through every guidebook. In so inhospitable a territory, who could survive, much less the typical carefree tourist? Both at the start of the novel and several times afterward, the narrator takes pleasure in seeing how that hapless hiker must undergo countless physical and mental tortures. At one point, the traveler despairs when he senses that his apparent forward progress only sets him further from his goal; at another point, he resigns himself to serve as carrion for the crows.[7] When he does not fall victim to the old guardian of the hills (p. 10) or to the topography of Región (p. 42), he loses the trail he needs to keep himself oriented (p. 52), or by night he hears noises, sees lights, and suffers pains of unknown origins (pp. 215–16).

In Región, nature is part of a hostile reality in which man is superfluous. The harshness of the land and the wildness of its surface stem from a climate of extreme heat and cold. To express this crude fact, Benet, like a present-day Homer, may adapt to his purposes ancient mythology, as when he calls the March wind a hostile Boreas, "que sabe. . . colocar sobre la cubierta de un corralón dos metros de nieve, sepultando animales, carros y personas" (p. 45). More often he invents his own myths. The effect is to place greater distance between the reality he describes and the reader's mental eye. Epic writers of both ancient and modern times deified and personified rivers, as in Luis de León's "Prophecy of the Tagus," imitating Horace. Benet humanizes the rivers of Región, especially the Formigoso "que, en comparación con su gemelo, observa desde su nacimiento una recta, disciplinada y ejemplar conducta para, sin necesidad de maestros, hacerse mayor de edad según el modelo establecido por sus padres y recipendarios" (p. 40). The inhabitants of Región, possessed by an atavistic fear, also excel at mythmaking. Like Dante in the wood of Christian suicides, whose spirits have assumed the form of bleeding trees (*Inferno*, Canto XIII), people living near the Torce River avoid contact with certain red flowers which, they say, contain the blood of patriarchs, kings, and Christian warriors (p. 189).

But the most terrifying myth of the region has for its protagonist the old guardian of the hills, Numa, whose name is also that of a legendary Roman king. Numa is the hero of this novelistic epic. Like an Achilles or an Aeneas, he bears upon his shoulders the destiny of his people. He belongs to the epic world because, to employ Benet's criterion, the human eye has never beheld him: "nadie se atreve a negar la existencia del hombre, al que nadie ha visto pero al que nadie tampoco ha podido llegar a ver" (p. 11). He has the attributes of a tutelary god, since he has the "don de la ubicuidad dentro de los límites de la propiedad que recorre día y noche con los ojos cerrados" (p. ll). He is the archetype of his breed of men: he is the "fiercest and most stubborn son" of the race of shepherds populating Región (p. 51). As befits an archetype, he lives in a world outside of time, although he guards the border between this mythical realm and the domain where history holds sway. It is his epic destiny to kill historical beings who venture into his sacred precinct, who profane it with their presence. It does not matter *how* Numa arrived at his antihistorical, semidivine status, and the theories

about his origin differ (p. 251). What is significant is his social function. It should not be forgotten that Benet is writing at a time when
the Franco regime boasts of having brought twenty-five years of
peace. Hence the disillusioned Dr. Sebastián may well be expressing Benet's own views when he ironically attributes the following
words to Numa: "Una paz, por muy ruin que sea, es siempre una
paz. Yo me cuido de mantenerla aquí al igual que vosotros la celáis
allá abajo" (p. 252). Numa, therefore, seems to embody racial purity, exempt from all criticism. He offers the neighbors of Región
the security of unchanging life, as opposed to the uncertainty of
risking hope in a future that could be better, but that could just as
likely turn out to be worse. Only in Numa, spirit of absolute stability, do all the people put their trust. As a result, if a truck from
the outside should disturb the quiet of the district, fifty neighbors
rush to the church steeple to await Numa's vengeance, the homi-
cidal shot that restores the peace (p. 14). Old women address their
laments to Numa and thereby forget for a while the ruins surrounding them (p. 20). Even Dr. Sebastián admits a certain superstitious
confidence in Numa as protector of his missing father (p. 144).
Moreover, Gamallo's daughter, who has returned to Región to recover the delight of times past, no sooner discovers the futility of
her return, than she hands herself over, at the end of the novel, to
Numa's cruelty. In this way, she, too, finds peace.

History, the foe of eternal Numa, has no place in Región. In
Sebastián's words, "no hay duda, es el Tiempo lo que todavía no
hemos acertado a comprender; es en el tiempo donde no hemos
aprendido a existir" (p. 252). As a consequence, the Civil War in
Región does not deserve consideration as anything but a mock epic.
It brings to view all the social evils that Benet criticized in "La entrada en la taberna." In Región, a people without any will or hope
coexist with a state aiming to control it for its own petty interests.
The narrator quite frankly reports that the Fascist victory represents a "return to statism" (p. 77). Because a vile egotism motivates
the military leaders, in Región the Civil War amounts to "una paradigma a escala menor y a un ritmo más lento de los sucesos penin-
sulares; su desarrollo se asemeja al despliegue de imágenes salt-
arinas de esa película que al ser proyectada a una velocidad más

lenta que la idónea pierde intensidad, colorido y contrastes" (p. 75). The mock epic simile, in agreement with Benet's aesthetic doctrine, clearly shows the scale of the comparison here in question. But it also points to the cause of the sluggish rhythm that characterizes the war in Región: the personal animosity of Colonel Gamallo, who fights for no ideal, but merely for the purpose of avenging himself on the territory where he has lost his adulterous wife and his honor (p. 67). When he inordinately prolongs his campaign against Región, he deprives it of all epic grandeur. Yet even had he been of nobler character, the lackluster quality of his enemy, the people of Región, would still have mired the war in sordid trivialities. The first Republican drive against the Nationalists in Región is less a struggle between armies than "la lucha entre. . . dos caravanas de coches y camiones anticuados" (pp. 35–36). In other epics, the poet proudly enumerates the warriors and the arms they brandish. In *Volverás a Región* the enumeration unfolds with an ironic barb. The narrator mocks the Republican infantry of Región, so poorly armed, that it seems to have stepped out of "una estampa de Epinal, de una vitrina de museo o de un desfile de viejas y alborotadas glorias; campesinos calzados con alpargatas y salomónicos cacherulos en la cabeza, armados con los viejos Mannlicher de la primera guerra de Africa, junto a los milicianos de gorrillo azul y mucha cartuchera, el casco ladeado y el barbuquejo caído. . .y los herméticos extranjeros de las brigadas. . .en cuyas caras ya había desaparecido, tras un año de combates, la sonrisa de la arribada para ser sustituida por la mueca del deber" (pp. 57–58).

As Hermann Cohen has noted,[8] the genuine epic poet takes it upon himself to rise above party allegiances in the hope of presenting a universal image of the events he must narrate; and Juan Benet writes with a suitable degree of impartiality: he has mocked the forces of the Republic, and he reserves sarcasm for the Fascist state. First he amasses epic epithets as if in imitation of the war poet Miguel Hernández;[9] afterward, he alludes to the petty thirst for vengeance in the conquering army. Colonel Gamallo's troops include "navarros entusiastas y pugnaces, de vallisoletanos de honra y flemáticos y reticentes gallegos cuyos nombres se inscribieron en unas cuantas cruces y lápidas de mármol, los ornamentos con que el nuevo Estado se decidió a pagar la destruccíon que había acarreado a aquella comarca refractaria a su credo" (pp. 65 – 66). In describing the Republican retreat amidst a dazzling shower of blue flares, Benet employs a complex epic simile that shows his skill in depicting frozen motion against a backdrop of war. He presents the retreating soldiers, suddenly illuminated, as "insectos hacia el zócalo cuando repentinamente se enciende la luz delatora, la respiración contenida, la mirada como las antenas paralizadas en un simulacro mortuorio, el dedo cerrado en el gatillo en actitud expectante" (p. 288). Here the reader's mind quickly swings between the unaccustomed world of the battlefield and the everyday world populated by insects. The juxtaposition of the two planes results in an overlapping of impressions that reduces the fighters in their paralysis and dread to the size of insects. In the background of a ludicrous war that is coming to an end, the sounds of an old gramophone are heard, perhaps Benet's symbol of the endless repetition of the same old song of centuries of warfare without consequence in the territory of Región (pp. 290 – 91).

In a land of such limited possibilities, Dr. Sebastián reflects, "El presente ya pasó y todo lo que nos queda es lo que un día no pasó; el pasado tampoco es lo que fue, sino lo que no fue; sólo el futuro, lo que nos queda, es lo que ha sido" (p. 245). Therefore time has a circular movement without end and embraces the void surrounding everyone (pp. 245 – 46). Dr. Sebastián's father has lived under the power of a telegraph wheel, his wheel of fortune. From him his son has inherited a defeatist's fatalism (p. 122). Both, endowed with passive characters, have suffered misfortunes in love: Dr. Sebastián's mother paralyzed her husband's will and stifled his emotion by vainly exhorting him to regain for the family the respectability she imagined as her birthright. Their house resembles that of a "héroe que convertida en museo y defendida por un cordón de seda es conservada en el mismo estado en que la dejó cuando tuvo que partir. . .para guerrear en Ultramar" (p. 119). This family hero "quizá no existió jamás" (p. 120). Hence, he, too, partakes of an epic essence. But Dr. Sebastián, as weak-willed as his father, enjoys as little success in his work and in his sentimental life. He marries a woman whom he abandons, allowing her to die without ever having sexual relations with her. Like Penelope, she spends twenty years—precisely the amount of time that Ulysses was away from Ithaca—"tejiendo durante todo el tiempo que estuvo casada, multiplicando por doquier su bordado ingenuo para llenar las horas que su marido la dejó sola" (p. 106). Why the lack of energy in her Ulysses? Just as, on the public plane, the state robs the people of fidelity to itself, so on the private plane, according to Sebastián, the family deprives the individual of selfhood (pp. 137, 139). Every obligation that guides man toward the future, toward progress, in Sebastián's opinion, unbalances the mind. Such is the mental ailment that this doctor diagnoses in his countrymen; and Numa, or the force of collective repression, forms the "prodrome" of that illness. Sebastián complains that in his country, the individual is cast aside while "su sociedad, su religión, su estado, y su silencio" (p. 222) are valued too highly.

In this antisocial protest, Sebastián is joined by the daughter of Colonel Gamallo. She might have been the noble heroine of a tragedy. Instead, she always ends up taking part in a comedy. This fate, after all, is to be expected in a novel definable as an epic in a paralytic state. For like Cohen or Ortega y Gasset, Benet conceives the novel as a critique of the epic.[10] Is it not reasonable to suppose, therefore, that like Cohen and Ortega, Benet views comedy as a critique of tragedy? This supposition acquires support from the life of Gamallo's daughter, who in her disillusionment recalls the Civil War as a mere "pretexto, el ardid que el destino impone, como a Ifigenia, para probar el apego a su padre" (pp. 158–59). If this new Iphigenia, urged by her father, had been able to give her life gladly for her country, then, with the danger behind her, she might have lived in peace with herself in a society "dispuesta a acoger [la] como una mártir" (p. 159). But she well knows the impossibility of her martyrdom. She has been deficient in ideals, filial affection, and a sense of duty (p. 278). The idealism she attributes to her father's generation (an idealism alien, of course, to him, as we have seen) has diminished for her own generation into an "object of irony" (p. 262). Educated in a middle-class milieu whose falseness she found apparent, she has grown up with the sensation of playing in a comedy, whose humorous situations she knew by heart, even though she did not know the whole argument of the play (p. 261). In other words, she has sought in vain the meaning of her life in general and, within it, of the civil war, which has taken away from her her innocence, her father, her lover, and her future. As the hostage of the Republicans during the war, she has questioned the value of the telephone call from her father, head of the Nationalist forces, who tried to appeal to emotions that she had never felt and to filial duties unknown to her. In general, Gamallo's daughter has deemed "unfortunate" the influence of all authority upon her, whether in the form of the female comrade who guarded her during the war, the procuress of the brothel in which she found herself after the war, or the domineering mother-in-law who marred the period of her marriage (pp. 274–77). In sum, since girlhood, she has deeply felt a sense of orphanhood, and in this feeling of being abandoned and alone she has grown to maturity.

How little she differs from the nearsighted youth whose mother left him at the outbreak of the war, and who lives obsessed with her absence! Since the abandoned son has never acquired the use of reason, he perceives the paralyzed epic of the war as a series of isolated impressions, as devoid of meaning for him as it is for Gamallo's daughter. The impressions themselves could hardly be more painful. Aside from the anxiety and fear of being alone, he experiences dread at the parades and demonstrations in the war, seen from the window. He yearns for some small hope for the future when he hears the servant woman recount bloody old tales of Moors and Christians, or when he sees, descending from the mountain, the vehicle transporting the war dead. Into a single image Benet condenses all the consequences of his motionless epic as he describes "un carruaje fúnebre y grotesco, devuelto por la sierra como los restos de un naufragio por la marea, cargado con los restos mortales de todos los antepasados deslumbrados por su propia ambición, conducido por un postillón borracho o un cadáver o un par de mulas enloquecidas" (p. 20). The allusion to the shipwrecked warriors recalls the Odyssey; the bedazzlement of the dead suggests their blindness in life to the reality surrounding them; the agelessness of the funeral cargo seems to hint at the failure of Spanish history; and the drunkenness of the postboy introduces this unhappy epic into the tavern of disillusion.

With such a spectacle before his eyes, for what can the orphan hope? He invents his own law as he endlessly devotes himself to his solitary game. According to an ironic Benet, the game lasts more years than the war itself (p. 178). In passing, Dr. Sebastián views God as a "Player" who gives men "free time without measure" in a landscape filled with ruins (p. 246). The vision of God the Player, present in Heraclitus' aphorisms, is not unknown to Homer.[11] But whereas in the classical epic men die as playthings of the gods, in *Volverás a Región* Dr. Sebastián succumbs at the hands of the orphan, who makes him his "doll" because, in his madness, the youth supposes that his victim has kept him from reuniting with his mother (p. 314). The past, therefore, succumbs to the future, which is the obsessive recollection of what has gone by, and time forms a circle in Región.

In a recent interview, Benet quoted a phrase from Faulkner as an Einsteinian law of the universe of memory: "Memory believes before knowledge remembers."[12] In *Volverás a Región* there appears a clear reminiscence of the phrase: "No es la memoria la que odia; es ciertamente la que cree, la que diez o veinte años más tarde se complace en presentar a una razón sin recuerdos todo un balance . . . de esperanzas frustradas" (p. 19). Like the orphan in the novel who yearns for even a fleeting hope of his mother's return, Benet as a child, separated from his parents during the war, doubtlessly felt helpless.[13] Without hope he must have devoted himself to the games of his fantasy, and it is possible that the bitter taste, the futility of waiting, has persisted in the games of his adult imagination. The persistence of his memory may account for the epic impartiality with which he presents the war, without enthusiasm for either of the contenders. The bitterness of remembering may also explain his painstaking care in portraying his epic in a paralytic state.

To summarize, *Volverás* has much in common with the start of the *Odyssey*, Book II: the hero remains absent (Numa); the house stays in ruins (Región), its inhabitants helpless. Other aspects of the novel—descriptions of nature and many war scenes—take on an epic or mock-epic tone. Although epic elements are more in evidence here than in other works of Benet, by no means do they disappear from his production. In *Una meditación* (1970), the narrator stresses the illness of ease, ill will, and vengeful spirit prevailing in postwar Región. Here the victorious Fascists take pleasure in glorifying their epic deeds and in insulting the vanquished. In the novel, as David K. Herzberger writes, Benet criticizes Fascism for paralyzing society with ideologies invented to cure its wounds.[14] In the short novel *Una tumba* (1971), the spirit of a dead officer plays a major role; like Gamallo, he represents a repressive force in Región. In *Un viaje de invierno* (1972), Benet once more seems to bring into play classical mythology, in which the goddess Demeter reveals mysteries to mortals while she awaits the return of spring and of her daughter Coré. However, by situating the novel in Región, where the passage of time is suspended, the author defers the coming of springtime indefinitely. In conclusion, therefore, Benet's relationship to classical literature may well provide us, as Ariadne did Perseus, a thread to guide us to the center of these twentieth-century literary labyrinths if, as critics, we have the almost epic temerity to enter them.

STEPHEN J. SUMMERHILL

# Prohibition and Transgression in *"Volverás a Región"* and *"Una meditación"*

It is almost a commonplace to say that Benet's is a fictional world built upon doubt, uncertainty, and an awareness of mystery. Ricardo Gullón has called *Volverás a Región* (1967) an effort to "recuperar un mundo ignorado, enigmático, extraviado en las nieblas del olvido";[1] while Marisa Martínez-Lázaro has seen *Una meditación* (1970) as a "narración fundamentada en la incertidumbre."[2] When reading a Benet novel, it is impossible not to be overwhelmed by an all-pervading sense that the represented reality is felt to contain forces that cannot be explained and that will always escape attempts at analysis. Benet himself has suggested as much. When asked what concerned him in his literature, he replied: ". . . el problema de siempre: que todo lo que nos rodea es un enigma. Mañana se puede poner a volar este sillón, ¿por qué no? Y seguimos sabiendo tan poco sobre nuestra propia naturaleza como en los días de la tragedia griega; o menos, quizá porque el hombre ya es más complejo."[3]

On the other hand, Benet has also said that we must not lose "la capacidad de introducir una cierta luz dubitativa en las sombras."[4] By this, he seems to mean that it is not sufficient merely to create a sense of the mysterious or inexplicable; it is also necessary to reach a certain understanding of the mystery, a perhaps tentative, never self-secure thread of meaning around which the light of knowledge can develop. In other words, the notion of mystery has two sides: to write in such a way as to give the reader a sense of events and mo-

tives that are enigmatic; yet at the same time, and equally important, to provide a hint of direction through which one might also
grasp meaning. And if this is so, we cannot be content to pass over
all the enigmas of Benet's work as simply inexplicable; we must also
take the risk of looking for their coherence. In what follows, I
would like to consider this other direction of Benet's work, that of
meaning, by analyzing *Volverás a Región* and *Una meditación* from
the point of view of the motives and behavior of the characters. The
world of Región, where almost all his fiction is set, is inhabited by
many strange kinds of characters, some of them apparently supernatural, and all of them immersed in intricate patterns of behavior
that at times seem to defy explanation. Much of what happens,
moreover, is submerged under a minute dissection of the reasons
for the characters' behavior; and often these reasons are more complicated than the actual behavior itself. *Una meditación*, for example, could be taken as a story about a group of mediocre and uninteresting people to whom little of note happens over a period of
some twenty-five years. And yet, through the complex meditations
of the narrator, a whole mythology of passion and fear is woven
about them, and their ordinariness is transformed into a mysterious, perhaps archetypal pattern of human destiny. The procedure,
we might say, is exactly the reverse of that used by Sánchez Ferlosio
in *El Jarama*, where mediocrity is stripped bare and left to speak for
itself. In Benet, it is embellished into a myth; it is subjected to the
hermeneutical power of the word and thereby transfigured into a
mysterious pattern of life.[5] That we should distrust and therefore
doubt such interpreting may be Benet's final, contradictory point.
But that does not prevent us from seeing it as an inner coherence
around which, even insecurely, his novels are constructed. It is this
coherence that I should like to bring out here.

Let us begin with what is perhaps the most emblematic case of
mystery in Benet, the strange character called Numa, who appears
above all in *Volverás a Región*. Numa is, of course, the guardian of
the forest, the enigmatic supernatural being who stalks the woods
outside Región, and kills anyone crossing an ancient "No Trespassing" sign placed in an apparently arbitrary spot deep in the moun-
tainous terrain. We are told that he has been in the forest since long

before anyone remembers; and yet, despite—or perhaps because of—the fact that he is everywhere within his mysterious protectorate, we know also that he has never been seen. No proof of his gunshots has ever been established, and the fact that his "infallible aim" cuts down any "tired soul" who crosses the barrier to his land is accepted unquestioningly, as something both necessary and indemonstrable, to be believed with neither explanations nor perplexity.[6] At the end of the novel it is Numa who hears Daniel Sebastián's invocation to keep things as they are and not to let Gamallo's daughter leave; for the novel closes with the sound of a distant gunshot that "vino a restablecer el silencio habitual del lugar" (p. 315).

This already tells us quite a bit about the character, but we might also recall that Numa is described as an "encarnación de una voluntad que duerme a la intemperie, dispuesta a despertar al primer sonido extraño" (p. 181). Moreover, "Quizá no existe sino como cristalización del temor o como la fórmula que describe (y justifica) la composición del residuo de un cuerpo del que se sublimaron todos los deseos" (p. 221). And finally, we recall that at one point, Numa speaks in the novel (or more likely, is imagined by Sebastián as speaking), and says that it is clear the people want him there. What he gives them is peace and tranquillity, while asking in return only that they hope for nothing more than punishment for any transgressor (p. 252).

Criticism has interpreted Numa as symbolic of "Franco y sus seguidores," as Manuel Durán puts it.[7] One might, however, pursue another, not necessarily contradictory, line of thought by considering the many suggestions that he may not even exist. If all the characters of the novel accept Numa unquestioningly without, however, ever having seen him, the implication is that the narration is drawing a careful distinction between his type of existence and that of everyone else. In effect, he seems to be presented as a fiction within a fiction, that is, not as a character like the other characters in the story, but as an imaginary being who has been created collectively by the people of Región in an effort to shun nature. The inhabitants of Región seem to intuit nature as a menacing, potentially uncontrollable force, a kind of blind, passionate will beyond their power ("una voluntad que duerme a la intemperie"), which is capable of destroying them if they come under its grasp. This *nature* or *passion*, the novel suggests, exists primarily in men, but it is feared so much that it has been projected imaginatively outside society in the form of a supernatural gunman protecting a prohibited zone. The threatening force is thus exiled from society to a place where it can do no immediate harm, and thereby serves as a gesture of self-protection, an attempt to increase their chances of survival. In consequence, Numa has an ambiguous role. As threat, he induces the people to stay in place because of the potential harm that could come to them were they to transgress the barrier to his world, that is, were they to give in to their own urge to passion. On the other hand, he also protects them, not only because he, as passion, is neutralized through exile, but also because he is presumed to eliminate those who might threaten society by allowing nature to dominate their lives. This explains why he is described in a contradictory manner as both source of peace and as a menace, for in fact he is both a protection and a threat.

What we have in Numa, then, is a whole way of life, an animistic symbol that expresses a conflict in the characters between, on the one hand, nature or passion, and on the other, society. The inhabitants of Región appear to have inherited and maintained a society from which passion (or "nature" or "instinct") is banned because it is feared. For them, to surrender oneself to passion is equivalent to transgressing a barrier into a forbidden or taboo zone of existence, and anyone who dares violate the prohibition, either by responding to passion within themselves or—in what symbolically amounts to the same thing—by venturing outside society beyond the warning sign and into nature, is deemed a transgressor who must be punished.

On the other hand, the fact that such a severe ban should even have to be made, the fact that passion should provoke so much fear that it has to be placed beyond limits, indicates that it must be felt to exercise a strong temptation. There could be no fear of this blind will unless it held some kind of attraction, even if only to a few, just as Numa could not continue to exist if men did not presume that every now and then, someone would attempt to cross over the warning sign and have to be shot. Thus, the people of Región must be irremediably drawn to passion, and it is this that makes them so fearful. Caught between personal desire and social ban, life is an irresolvable struggle between passion and society, transgression and prohibition.

Seen in this light, Numa synthesizes much of the drama of Benet's characters and can therefore help to clarify much of their apparently enigmatic behavior. Fundamentally, both *Volverás a Región* and *Una meditación* describe how at least two, but ultimately many, generations of Spaniards have lived under the deadening weight of the same kind of conflict that produced Numa. They have been trapped between the social restrictions placed upon their passions and their deeply felt urge to violate these restrictions in search of freedom, self, and love. The contradiction is that they know themselves to be the origin of restriction, and yet they also feel unable either to accept it completely or to surmount it. They want to escape and they do not want to. They constantly push against the barriers of society, yet they are perpetually afraid of doing so, and therefore never really make much of an effort. This leads almost inevitably to a personal sense of failure, as sooner or later they give up hope for the future and spend their lives looking back in frustration upon the nonfulfillment of the past. It is this failure, the ultimate inability of any person to break the fatal deadlock between prohibition and transgression, either by breaking with society in favor of the self or by accepting society and forgetting about the self, that seems to be one of the primary sources of the theme of ruin that underlies so much of Benet's work. In a world structured upon an irremediable opposition between passion and society, there seems no final answer but a fatalistic recognition that fear will always win out while leaving ruin and decay as the ultimate product of man's passage.

We may see this more closely by analyzing the two main characters of *Volverás a Región*, Marré Gamallo and Daniel Sebastián. In the case of the former, we have a woman who has lived a perpetual coming and going between a desire for sexual freedom and a fear of it. Her restrictive education during the years of the Republic provoked her desire to explore sexuality upon leaving school; but for two years, she was paralyzed by her fear of it (pp. 260–61). When society collapsed in the Civil War, she did achieve a brief instant of self-fulfillment through her love with the godson of Sebastián. He, however, was soon killed, as if pleasure led inevitably to punishment, or at least the condemnation to be ephemeral. Back in postwar society, Marré lived a socially acceptable life, married and wealthy, with the small transgressions permitted by society, such as adultery; yet she always felt a deep desire to break with all decency (p. 158). However, it was this that she felt unable to do for many years. Finally, she has come back to Región in a last attempt to abandon her routine married life and develop a common bond with Sebastián, the godfather of her long lost lover. Struggling for many years between a desire for passion and an all-pervasive fear of it, she has at last been able to conquer the latter by abandoning acceptability and acknowledging that only her passionate experience of youth was ever worthwhile.

As for Sebastián, he too had the same restrictive upbringing, and this made him resent the key institution of society, the family. He sees the family as a "struggle for stability" (p. 134) that amputates passions because they are sensed as unstable (p. 138). Any family member who does not conform, or who tries to reserve a piece of his life for himself, he says, will be punished; for family is but the "trap of reason" whose sole purpose is to hide man from his "demon," passion. Just as in the case of Marré Gamallo, then, Sebastián's prohibitory background creates a sense of the priority of passion and a desire to express the urges that have been socially repressed.

And yet, even more than Marré Gamallo, who eventually does manage to break with society, even temporarily, Sebastián lacks all courage to transgress. His feeble effort to flee with María Timoner many years ago was marked above all by fear to take the final step; and his reaction when he lost her was to marry a woman whom he had no intention of loving and with whom he would forever refuse to engage in sexual intercourse throughout many years of married life. It is as if he had become so embittered by his inability to transgress that he decided to give in completely to society and carry its prohibition against passion to an extreme. By so doing, Sebastián comes to epitomize all the contradictions of Región. He resents society, opposes its ban upon passion; but at the same time, he is fatalistically resigned to its domination over life. Indeed, he even comes to need prohibition, for he knows that the return of Marré Gamallo threatens to let passion loose upon Región: by coming back, she is attempting to transgress society and must be punished. So, in his last defense, he calls upon Numa to destroy her. For him, all transgression causes merely a passing upset that was already doomed to failure, and he prefers to hasten the collapse rather than join this woman in still another futile effort to love.

In general, then, *Volverás a Región* can be said to develop around an opposition between an older and a younger generation, that of Sebastián and that of Marré Gamallo. Both believe passion to be primary in their lives; both reject the prohibitions of society against it; and both are characterized above all by an ever-present fear of transgression. On the other hand, each adopts a different way of living with it: Marré Gamallo struggles unsuccessfully to overcome the barriers to passion, while Sebastián has long since chosen to keep them intact.

It is significant that in both these cases, as in those of other characters who fit this pattern,[8] the narration gives considerable emphasis to childhood, particularly the restrictive and confining aspects of upbringing. Childhood is a complex leitmotiv throughout Benet, partly because it suggests an ideal state of spontaneous instinct, and especially because it is the period of socialization when the adult strips the child of his or her natural (or "instinctive") urges and thereby perpetuates the dilemma of repression. In *Volverás a Región*, childhood is present not only in the references to the early years of the characters, but also in the lonely boy who is abandoned by his mother during the Civil War, becomes locked in an infantilistic wait for her return, and now, many years later, mistakenly believes Marré to be the mother so long awaited. Like Numa, this child is a symbol related to the dialectic between prohibition and transgression. On the one hand, he is the hopelessness of all innocence and passion in this antinatural world. At the same time, he is the son whom Marré Gamallo never had with her lover, and therefore a vision of the frustration of their passion, and of the impossi-

ble bond that might have been created between her and Sebastián.
And finally, he is a symbol of the futility of, yet moral right to all
transgression; for in a final rage of hopeless passion, he kills the
character most representative of prohibition, Sebastián.[9]

It is difficult not to sense in many of these ideas a rather basic
Freudian view of existence. It is not necessarily that Benet is en-
gaged in an artificial transference of psychoanalytic theory to his
fictional world, but that there seems to be a general coincidence of
attitude. The preeminence of sexuality, for example, as the major
form that passion takes, and the general sense that the conflict between individual and society is a perpetual structure of existence
seem very close to Freud. If we recall, moreover, that Benet himself
says that the idea for Numa occurred to him from a reading of *The
Golden Bough*,[10] and that Frazer's monumental work profoundly
influenced Freud's *Totem and Taboo*, we can begin to judge the general background of his ideas. In a very real sense, Benet is contributing to the very myth that Freud perpetuated, that of man's "eternal"
urge and fear to express libidinal instincts.[11]

On the other hand, *Volverás a Región* is not really concerned
with the details of Freudian theory, for Benet seems much more interested in presenting a whole fictional world with its history and
rich natural landscape.[12] This impression changes, however, as soon
as we encounter *Una meditación,* where one has a far clearer sense
that Freud is being used by a first-person narrator in order to explain a collective behavior. *Una meditación* is a complex and difficult novel because, in the end, we cannot even be sure that any of
the characters ever existed outside the mind of the narrator, whose
ideas about the opposition between prohibition and transgression
form the ideological nucleus of the text. Essentially, the novel is one
man's discourse on the inability of every person to violate society
through passion; and the particulars of the story—the fragments of
plot, the characters who pass in and out—could well have been developed after the fact in order to exemplify the theory. Benet has
warned us to be sensitive to the ambiguities of unreliable narration
in this work, a hint that the narrator's mania for interpreting the
lives of others should not be altogether trusted.[13] Perhaps there is an

ironic distance between the interpretation and the reality of the events themselves, a fact which, because we are entirely dependent upon the narrator, could only be verified by "reading between the lines" and apprehending a subterrranean world different from that which is presented to us. As suggested earlier, this might lie in the overall mediocrity of the characters. Although there are definite examples of pathological or "exceptional" behavior (Jorge Ruan, for example, who douses rats with gasoline so as to determine how far they "shoot" when lit), the figures who populate *Una meditación* are remarkably undistinguished, hardly deserving of the passionate motives attributed to them. Is it, then, the mythifying hermeneutics of Freud that is itself being ironized? Are we to read the dialectic between prohibition and transgression as an idle embellishment of an uninteresting reality? Even this is unclear because the dialectic does not falsify or conceal the characters' mediocrity. Rather, it accounts for it by finding underlying motives. In any case, the possibility that the narrator should be understood ironically prevents us from reaching a definitive conclusion that Benet actually *believes* the dialectic himself. I shall try to suggest some implications of this at the end.

It is significant that *Una meditación* itself begins with a long introduction on the family life of most of the characters when they were children before the outbreak of the Civil War. As in the earlier novel, what is important here is the socialization process undergone by the young person. With a fine eye for the little hypocrisies of daily life, the narrator presents a group of adults who put passion first in their lives, but who make great efforts to conceal this fact from public view. This cuts them off from each other, and creates a life of loneliness and isolation that contrasts sharply with the spontaneous and communal lives of the children. Because the latter are constantly reprimanded, however, and because they tend to imitate their elders, they gradually, almost inevitably, learn to repress their spontaneity and live in the dual world of the adult: to live behind the facade of "decent society," and to seek out pleasure from one's passions in secret. Only when they have thus become hypocrites like their parents, when they have acquired this irresolvable conflict between prohibition and transgression, only then can they be said to have become adults. In the novel, this coincides with the outbreak of the Civil War.

What follows is a series of haphazardly narrated reminiscences about these and other children with similar backgrounds during their adult life after the Civil War. In this main part of the novel, we see various couples pulled by the force of passion to seek sexual contact with one another. The narrator presents each experience as an entry into a dangerous "zone of shadows" inside the self, and identifiable with a long lost moment of early childhood when the self felt securely protected by a maternal presence. As the characters enter the danger zone, however, that is, as they start to come up against psychological barriers equivalent to Numa's "No Trespassing" sign, fear begins to take over. They sense an insecurity about themselves and feel that the carnal relationship with another is only going to bring them pain. And at this point, they take a fatal step. They call upon their reason to explain to them why this pain must result. But as the narrator constantly insists, reason is in opposition to the body. It is dependent upon fear, and its function is to mitigate the pain of passion by erecting social norms against it. Specifically, the central norm of reason is a prohibition against incest in opposition to the desire of the individual to find a state of pleasure similar to that of dependency upon the mother. This norm is what ultimately prevents a complete surrender of the individual to passion. Fearful to cross this last barrier called reason, fearful to enter fully into the zone of shadows where self and passion might finally be liberated with the other, the characters concede a basic impossibility in all transgression and withdraw back into loneliness within the at least safe confines of society. The price for such failure is high. The characters—or the narrator for them—sense that they have ritually sacrificed their most intimate self to the stability of a "nonlife" on this side of the barrier. In this context, the entire novel can be seen as representing a highly stylized and mythical *sacrifice* in which each person is immolated on the altar of society.[14]

It will be sufficient to mention only a few of the most important examples of this pattern as they appear in the work. There are "mi prima Mary" and Carlos Bonaval, who run off together in a rapture of passion during the first days of the Civil War. After a few weeks together, Carlos realizes that he is not opposed to received principles, and he decides to disengage himself from the affair. He had caught a first glimpse of perversion, we are told, and, fearing a commitment to it, preferred a life within society.[15] For her part, Mary seems forever disillusioned by this initial failure. She quickly marries another (Julián), goes into exile, divorces, remarries, and returns to Spain many years later, now terminally ill. At the end of her life, she looks back and concludes that prohibition has no limits and that her struggle against it has been futile (pp. 117–19).

Then there is the case of Emilio Ruiz, the staunchest defender of social codes in the work, who is, however, unable to live by them more than a few weeks at a time without feeling compelled to break them (pp. 187–88). He becomes entangled between what are called "phallic" and "cephalic" impulses toward Leo (that is, Laura): on the one hand, he wants to explore the "paramaternal cave" of her body, while on the other, he feels the pressure of norms against incest (p. 197). His answer is to look for a "solución de compromiso entre el respeto y la violación" (p. 134) by turning to the hotel proprietress and, fearful to the point of trembling, succumbing to orgasm outside her bedroom door. At no point can he resolve his desire for passion, nor his fear of it.

One could accumulate many more examples of the pattern. In the end, the following words of Tío Ricardo, who is characterized as an oracle with a special awareness of reality (p. 42), seem to summarize the text:

Volvemos siempre a lo mismo; es y será el miedo lo que nos enseña lo que somos y lo que nos impide ver lo que podemos ser. Frente a nosotros— y no necesariamente definida por esa cadena de montañas—existe una zona ciega que nadie se atreve a cruzar . . . . [Te hablo] en nombre de todos los que nos hemos mantenido aquí, respetando la limitación, sin otro consuelo que el de la supervivencia . . . . Todo lo que les hemos podido ofrecer es esto: una tierra de la que escapar. Ciertamente sólo lo logrará quien esté dispuesto a atravesar esa zona ciega, sin cuidarse de saber qué clase de sorpresa le va a deparar. Porque los que seguimos aquí, aceptando tales limitaciones, en realidad no vivimos; nos conformamos con saber que estamos vivos. (p. 259)

In *Una meditación*, two characters, Enrique Ruan and Cayetano Corral, actually cross into the zone of shadows, but they are never heard from again. Passion is incompatible with society, and the rest must learn to be content with knowing that, though they do not live, they are at least alive.

At the outset, it was noted that Benet wants to put a certain "luz dubitativa" in his texts as a kind of organizing principle through which the apparently mysterious events of his novels might be at least partly understood. Without meaning to reduce his works to a simple exposition of such a theme, it seems possible to suggest that the opposition outlined here between prohibition and transgression fulfills this function and that it enables the reader to naturalize or conventionalize what are among the most difficult novels to come out of Spain in many years.[16] It is not that mystery is thereby eliminated in the fictional world of Región, but that it is given a frame of reference within which to grasp many of its various manifestations in the texts.

One could of course go further than this and say that the whole idea stands as Benet's interpretation of both Spanish society and even of all of Spanish history.[17] Such a *realistic* reading presents no major obstacles as long as it is remembered that the distinctive feature of Benet's work is to take a firmly antirealistic stance and always to remind the reader that the ideas presented in his novels may be no more than pure language whose value, as ideas, is perhaps nil.[18] In other words, what really seems to count in this work is the actual construction of the text itself, the stylistic elaboration of an intermediary zone where the text can be seen as a construct of meaning without, however, ever appearing either as a radically empty formal structure or as a fully coherent and therefore verisimilar symbol of reality.[19] Thus, if we find an opposition between prohibition and transgression in his novels, it is not necessarily because Benet is convinced that social and historical reality *is* that way, but perhaps for no other reason than that this rather "classical" conflict already exists in a widely known cultural context and can serve as a convenient formal device around which to organize his texts. At the same time, by stressing the very formality of the ideas, as, for example, in the complex discussion conducted so ritualistically by the characters or in the uncertain irony of the narrator in *Una meditación*, he reminds the reader of their artificiality and thereby calls attention to the construction of the novel. In this sense, Benet seems to incarnate very deliberately that peculiar state of "suspended" or "postponed" meaning ("sens suspendu"), which Roland Barthes has isolated as the essence of literature: he opens up a meaning about the world, and in the very act of offering it, he arrests it and prevents its completion by making us so cognizant of the tenuousness of it all.[20] This may be the final "luz dubitativa" to which his novels ultimately point: to leave us hanging in a perpetual uncertainty about whether the mysteries we encounter have really been clarified or whether they might not in fact have been made even more obscure than ever.

MARY S. VÁSQUEZ

# The Creative Task:
# Existential Self-Invention in "Una meditación"

*Una meditación*, published in 1970, is the second novel in Juan Benet's Región cycle. Set vaguely, though with the precision of the most exacting civil engineer, in the northwest of Spain, Región is, like Faulkner's Yoknapatawpha County or García Márquez's Macondo, a mythical area that comes to constitute a world, a microcosm of the human state. In *Una meditación*, however, even Región cedes in importance to the novel's major emphasis: the tracing of the narrator-protagonist's laborious task of existential self-creation. I propose to demonstrate here that this activity of self-invention, and the novel's disjointed chronicling of it, exemplifies the principal aspects of the existential dilemma: the situation of the narrator-protagonist, the nature of his self-imposed task, the terms forming its inescapable context, the nonlinear process through which the task is carried out, and the content of the imperfect creation attained. I will attempt to show that the baroque thematic elements and literary style serve to enhance the existential nature of the work. For purposes of this discussion I define existentialism as an attitude—as opposed to a doctrinal philosophy—that views man as irrevocably alone in an absurd universe, condemned to invent himself in order to give meaning both to self and to his world.

It is difficult to speak of a story line in *Una meditación*. There are, rather, anecdotal centers that function as interlocking series of concentric circles. Around these centers, characters and incidents are presented that recur, often in an altered context, as the narrator-protagonist explores through them the eccentricities and the sorrows of his own family, of the neighboring Ruan and Mazón clans, of other persons in the area linked by acquaintance or place. Grandson of a local entrepreneur and orphaned in the Civil War, the narrator returns numerous times to Región and now undertakes to interpret the content and characters of the anecdotal raw material.

I have employed the term "narrator-protagonist," though it is tempting to affirm with Gonzalo Sobejano[1] that *Una meditación* has no protagonist character, that the protagonist is, rather, Región—the sum, and more, of the fragments of interrelated lives the narrator attempts to reconstruct. Región, like Macondo and Yoknapatawpha, is indeed a world, with its themes of pettiness, rivalry, rejection, anesthetization and, through them, deeper themes of human struggle, waste, and failure—in the narrator's repeated term, ruin. That same narrator's posture of abstraction from the happenings to which he alludes and his chameleonlike nature as he moves from buried narrator to sententious diagnostician to omniscient "I" and back again all would seem to point away from a role of protagonist, of "first actor" in this novelistic world.

Yet there is a fundamental difference between the worlds of Macondo and Yoknapatawpha, on the one hand, and Región, on the other. Región is the anecdotal sum of the novel, but not its center. Región is the surrounding ambience to be defined, those who people it, the characters to be deciphered—however contradictorily—in the activity at the novel's center: the narrator's labor as meaning-giver, his existential task of self-creation. For the novel's action is mental activity—the narrator's mental activity. Creation is actually reconstruction, with memory as the recalcitrant agent that attempts to conjure up the past, not to mourn or celebrate it, but to interpret, to understand, to define that past's truth and, with it, that of the narrator within the past. The task is an impossible one. Were this not so, were the task to be fully realized, the existential nature of the novel would surely be diminished. Instead, the goals of the narrator's task are a pretext for contemplation of the process of such an undertaking, and the attempt at discovery—the narrator's action—quickly becomes more important than what is, and what cannot be, discovered. It is around this attempt that the novel's more important explicit and implicit thematic statements revolve, statements about the nature of cognition, the workings of memory and time, the impossibility of true knowing, the certainty only of failure.

The life of Región, then, becomes the material through which the narrator's action moves. Coupled with the deeper themes accompanying the concept of ruin, this life nourishes the subjective rememorative action and the implications arising from it. In this sense it is, I believe, appropriate to view the narrator as the novel's "first actor."

The joining of narrative and principal character functions in *Una meditación* underlines the existential nature of the storyteller both as active creator himself and as sole value-giver in a world devoid of any meaning other than that with which he is able to imbue it. The centrality of his action emphasizes the subjective frame of reference essential to a view that situates the individual in such a self-inventing role, while the nature of that action as thought suggests the abstraction with which the subjectivity of existentialism is in frequent tension. The narrator-protagonist duality, then, reinforces existential aspects of the narrator's situation, his task and its carrying out, its contextual terms and thematic implications.

The narrator's situation partakes of a number of markedly existential traits. First, like all humans, he is totally and irremediably alone. The victim, he reflects, whether of himself or an unnamed adversary, never knows whether or not he could have escaped his dilemma, "tal es su soledad." [2] His parents, too, are "reducidos a una soledad que conocían de sobra" (p. 48). For the narrator, their lack of communication is, clearly, the human state: "Dos personas que hablan y se entienden haciendo uso de las mismas palabras están a menudo viendo en su interior dos espectáculos diferentes, ninguno de los cuales emerge a la vista del otro y sólo de vez en cuando dan origen a una emoción compartida y análoga" (p. 51). Appropriately, there is no true dialogue in *Una meditación*; all quotations are monologues or fragments of them, and conversation is recorded only indirectly.

With no real access to those around him, and unable to depend

upon their versions of the chaos out of which he must attempt to
create, the narrator frequently suggests that man moves in a vac-
uum of which he catches occasional, horrifying glimpses. These
looks send him back to his solitary state in which, lacking either
given values or communication with others, his point of reference is
necessarily subjective. He is the existential, marginal man, ever at a
remove. Benet's narrator is present only silently at the events related
in the novel—if, indeed, he is present at all. More often he has recourse to such secondary and tertiary sources as old photographs or
hearsay. Or the omniscient "I" arbitrarily gains access to facts that
remain dubious. His alienation extends to his own sense of himself.
The narrator considers that he is both a self and a memory of self:
the two can never be fully reconciled. He meditates upon

> toda la estampa animada de un yo que en vano trataba de incorporar a
> mi memoria para convencerme de que sólo así podía estar seguro de vivir
> ahora, quedaba detenida y distanciada en un punto del atrás (como si entre
> mi yo y mi memoria del yo existiera siempre una distancia, aunque infini-
> tesimal, insalvable, la misma que separaba a Aquiles de la tortuga) para
> significar una vez más—y con tanto mayor dolor—la injusta y siniestra ex-
> clusión de un verdadero vivir que tal yo y tal imagen disfrutan y sufren fun-
> didos en uno, inseparables en la desgracia así como en el gozo. (p. 66)

As he conducts the process of attempted reconstruction of the
past—and of conciliation of self and its memory—the narrator employs the image of a viewer at a movie (p. 33). The metaphor is apt,
for the narrator, though actor as well, is, like the proverbial man
who was a guest at his own wedding, spectator of his own life.

Expressive of the narrator's sense of alienation is his self-mockery.
It is sometimes direct, as in his use of foreign words when they add
nothing of flavor or meaning that a Spanish term could not provide;
on other occasions indirect, as when the narrator moves from apparent paraphrase and subsequent quotation of a pompous or
preachy character into a serious and substantive reflection on the
same topic and back again into preachiness or open self-parody.

In fact, it is this alienation from self that leads the narrator to the
setting of his task: "Creo que un divorcio de esa especie infantiliza,
le lleva a un hombre a vivir en un permanente sinsabor, a pasar por
el mundo sin haber alcanzado el rango completo que le corresponde

y a temer, día tras día y hora tras hora, no lograr nunca ser, ausente del pensamiento y la memoria como tales, los testigos de cargo que con su sola presencia demuestran el dolor" (p. 66). Turning away from the fear to which his alienation and occasional glimpses of meaninglessness lead him, he sets out to investigate, to come to know, even to teach (the narrator refers to his "deseo de dar a conocer" [p. 77]). Yet his investigation leads him precisely back to the fear against which the only protection is the "parenthesis of ignorance" (p. 68) man places around himself, the narrator tells us. For the horror of knowing is the knowledge that one cannot truly know. In a world whose only motive force is chance, arbitrariness is total, and reasons do not exist. Although existential happenstance in *Una meditación* is counterpointed to fatality and often interchanged with it in the narrator's musings, the terms of the experience are purely existential. And precisely because of its totality, the experience of nothingness must often be reduced to a trivial reference, just as it is often induced by a trivial reality. Benet's narrator can be led to despair by a friend's failure to appear at the appointed hour, much like Francisco Ayala's character made despondent by a cup of cold coffee or like a character in Elena Quiroga's *Algo pasa en la calle* who when pressed for the reasons for his trauma is able only to repeat that "huele a cebolla." Because human effort is mocked by the imperviousness of an indifferent universe, trivialized by guaranteed defeat, the experience of human despair can be appropriately rendered in expressions of triviality. And just as each of the above characters is condemned to fail, each must start anew the process of creating against nothingness and create anew "el mismo todo anterior" (p. 52). As the novel's elliptical time movement suggests, there is no continuity. The character Cayetano Corral, who, the narrator tells us, loves whalelike women—but only two months out of the year—spends his days tinkering with clocks and charts. Cayetano makes continual notes on his thoughts, but he writes only with chalk and he erases everything.

If these, then, are the terms by which the narrator's task of self-invention is to be carried out, why undertake it at all? "Debe ser la facultad de toda especie dolida, que necesita saber en parte lo que fue . . . para vencer el dolor que le produce lo que es" (p. 52). As man is condemned to defeat, he is also condemned to create. The attempted performance of the narrator's task is, likewise, existential in nature: it is the struggle for self-invention of a lone individual; it is a subjective labor, situational rather than sequential. Yet, it is existential with a twist. The attempted invention focuses entirely on the past, and it becomes a more purposive stance than that of many existential characters, to whom, like Camus's Meursault, things simply happen.

The narrator's struggle is not only against meaninglessness and the certainty of failure—contextual terms of the struggle, as seen earlier—but, in the carrying out of the task, with both memory and time. Memory is the narrator's vehicle of creation. Obdurate, self-contradictory, ever unreliabe, it is, nonetheless, the best primary source the narrator has. In memory's convoluted workings, paralleled in the novel by the involved syntax and nearly endless sentences of unbroken narrative stream, names and deeper identities, as well as time periods, are blended and interchanged. Thus, at a superficial level, Leo is also Laura, while in deeper terms of identity she is also the narrator's cousin Mary, as her first husband Julián fuses with her second, and also with the neighbor Jorge Ruan, whose identity blends in turn with that of his brother Enrique. Images belonging to different time periods interpenetrate as well. Julián walking down the steps of Mary's home to go to war becomes Julián on the same steps years later, but also Mary's second husband awkwardly descending the stairs of the home where he is anathema. Similarly, the ribbon at the neck of Mary's blouse the day the narrator skins his knee as a child becomes the ribbon that the prostitute Rosa de Llanes lets fall when with the narrator in adulthood. In the reflection of memory's erratic nature, the narrator can recreate another character's monologue word for word, yet an unpopular suitor in the household is referred to as "aquel Emilio y algo así como Ruiz de algo" (p. 107) and his own grandfather is "apoderado, allegado, consejero o no sé qué, de una pequeña fábrica de vidrio soplado" (p. 7). When the narrator asks, "¿Cómo voy a saber de qué manera se inició aquella conversación?" (p. 199), we can almost hear his self-mocking indignation.

Equally difficult as his struggle with memory is the narrator's battle against a time that denies continuity yet moves characters inexorably toward ruin. The characters of *Una meditación* are fascinated with clocks and watches, yet they either do not believe in the efficacy of such devices—"solamente los desastres son capaces de fijar el tiempo" (p. 203)—or find themselves overpowered by them. When Cayetano Corral finally completes his reassembly of a clock, the device takes control of his workshop and destroys it. Fittingly, the novel's time is nonlinear. As in Martín-Santos's *Tiempo de silencio*, scenes succeed one another as series of static images, each of which, ironically, may bear a high emotional charge. Frequently, too, the content of one such static scene contradicts that of another. The consequence is most often the slow motion camera effect of Robbe-Grillet. Occasionally, an image is caught and held, like that of Mary's sweetheart departing for war. When such retention of an image does occur, the result is again ironic, for the contextual connotation is in such cases one of irreparable loss. Similarly, when time does move, forward movement traces a process of defeat. As in the characters' lives, waste and ruin provide the only continuity.

Allusion has been made to a number of elements of literary expression in *Una meditación*: narrative functions, characterization, syntactic qualities, manipulation of time, use of dialogue, narrative structure, imagery. These elements, both illustrative and creative of the novel's thematic statements, center around two opposed processes, separation and fusion. The functions of separation are in consonance with existential alienation, fragmentation, incommunication, disconformity. They emphasize the multiplicity within superficial unity, the broken nature of the apparently straight line. The technique of fusion in *Una meditación* is baroque in nature, replacing the frequent starkness of existential narrative with a rich multiplication of language and concept. By removing accepted but often artificial barriers of time, identity, and process, techniques of fusion join seemingly disparate elements in search of a fuller interpretation of reality.[3] Here, too, movement is nonlinear, lying, instead, in the tension between juxtaposed elements. The result is suggestive, by a different route, of the multiple and contradictory truth signaled by the separation techniques. In *Una meditación* the juxtapositions of truth / falseness, knowledge / ignorance, reality / fantasy, and abstraction / subjectivity are important elements of narrative structure. Of these, it is the counterpointing and union of abstraction / subjectivity that is most central to both theme and novelistic process. In it the separation and fusion techniques of *Una meditación* most closely meet. As they suggest a dual approach to an ever-elusive truth, they point as well to the two, often contradictory faces of existentialism: the state of existential alienation and the task of existential creation.

JULIA LUPINACCI WESCOTT

---

# Subversion of Character Conventions in Benet's Trilogy

If illusion is due to the interaction of clues and the
absence of contradictory evidence, the only way to fight
its transforming influence is to make the clues contradict
each other and to prevent a coherent image of reality from
destroying the pattern in the plane.

E. H. GOMBRICH[1]

Disparate modern theories of narrative often concur in their insistence that novels are about characters and that characters are "people."[2] Yet the structuralists have demonstrated that such a view is a
contingency, that such a posture characterizes only one type of
novel, the one Barthes has labeled "readerly."[3] The novels of Benet's
trilogy repeatedly affirm the structuralist position, for Benet structures these works in a way that impedes conventional readerly processing of character.[4] Examination of this breach of the "character
contract,"[5] and the concurrent existence of contrary novelistic conventions and assumptions about the nature of human "reality," will
be the focus of this essay.

Ducrot and Todorov outline the theoretical approaches to character from which we may extrapolate the conventions of character
enacted by the readerly novel, and in so doing they provide us with
a convenient summary of the tradition against which Benet works.
Briefly, the character is the "subject of the narrative proposition,"
while his attributes and actions constitute the predicate.[6] That is,
the novel is fundamentally a statement about its characters, their
ethical and ontological concerns. The character is the paradigm of

attributes that describe him. The reader infers these attributes from actions that must be different enough to warrant mention, and yet consistent enough so that the character is always recognizable. Formally, paradigmatic development distinguishes dynamic characters from static ones. Furthermore, importance of role and degree of complexity distinguish protagonists from secondary figures. Interrelationships among the characters can be formulated in terms of oppositions based on character attributes and actions. The dynamics of these relationships embody the syntagmatic structure of the novel.

The readerly novel principally assumes the coherence and intelligibility of the human psyche. Like the physical human being, the psychological and emotional being is a discrete entity of proportions apprehensible by the perceiving mind through observation and reasoning. The establishment of causal relationships permits the inference of the exact dimensions of that interior being from exterior clues. When E. M. Forster says that fictional characters can be fully understood because their "inner as well as their outer life can be exposed," he points to the accessibility of information about the psyche as the distinguishing feature between human and fictional beings, but he assumes the coherence of the psyche in both.[7] Indeterminacy is precluded as is the notion of extraneous information. All actions reveal traits; no information is resistant to this type of processing. The result is a "complete" personality, one in which the perceiver need tolerate no gaps. In short, the physical self, as it moves concretely through space and time, reveals another—hidden but no less circumscribed—self that is at any point the sum of all its preceding actions and thoughts. The inner being is coherent and intelligible because this summation can in fact be made. Its coherence and intelligibility are a function of its chronology.

This definition of character does not hold for the "character" in Benet's trilogy, who seems no longer to be "the means of our understanding and making sense of an ordered world."[8] Determination of a paradigm of traits is blocked: it is impossible to formulate a consistent pattern of character attributes from actions or statements. Rather, the predominant reaction fostered by Benet's "characters" is one of uncertainty: the reader does not know who they are, what they are like, the parameters of their story, nor why it is being told.[9] The physical being is related to no other parallel, clearly delimited, psychological self. That is, the character has lost its "human" qualities of intelligibility and coherence.

Traditional character formulation in Benet's trilogy is inhibited by means of several techniques. Reduction of the physical dimension of story (space and setting) is a factor that plays an important, if secondary, role in that inhibition. If a character's displacement of space is an indication of its physical reality, and if that physical reality itself is a precondition for and implication of a parallel interior self, withholding information of the physical aspects of a character must certainly undermine both. Hence the physical aspects of Benet's characters are never disclosed.[10] In *Volverás a Región*, for example, the woman, who appears to be significant because she is one of only two participants in a "dialogue" that lasts almost the entire novel, is never described physically. Indeed, her first entrance in the novel—traditionally requiring physical description—seems to undercut her physical reality by its indirect presentation: "En aquella ocasión no se trataba de una vieja camioneta cargada de bultos y cuerdas, sino de un coche negro, de modelo antiguo pero con empaque. No por eso, ni el hecho de ser conducido por una mujer. . . ."[11]

Her entrance is completed after a narratorial interruption of no less than sixty pages: "Toda la tarde lo estuvo observando desde lejos, detrás de una cerca de piedras, los ojos clavados en sus dos grandes faros, incapaz de curar con el recuerdo aquello que la memoria ha sellado con dolor; hasta que de improviso una mujer de elevada estatura apareció junto a él" (p. 89). Use of the verb *apareció* further detracts from the reader's sense of her physical being: she is almost incorporeal. The withholding of her name increases the reader's inability to gain a sense of her physical presence because, as Chatman has pointed out, "The proper name in this sense is precisely the identity or quintessence of selfhood."[12]

Fragmentation of events and the subsequent destruction of chronology is a major inhibitor of traditional character formation. As G. W. Allport has shown, "In order to know that any individual has a trait it is necessary to have evidence of repeated reactions."[13] Entanglement of events produced by fragmentation fosters precisely the opposite effect: it promotes reader uncertainty as to the very nature of the character's reactions as well as to their appropriateness.

Ambiguity in the narrative stance, the specific concern of this essay, is another major obstacle to conventional character development and provides a fruitful avenue of approach to new organizational patterns within the novel. Not only is presentation of the characters unclear, but the instrument of their representation, narration itself, ensures confusion, thereby redirecting attention away from the characters to the narrative itself. The reader, dependent on, yet unsure of, the narrative stance, is fundamentally uncertain about his own vantage point on the story, of which a chief component is character. Stylistic devices used throughout the trilogy support the ambiguity, which isolates the reader from the story. Each novel can be seen as a variation on ambiguity of narration, and all weave a web of conflicting clues that leave the reader uncertain even about the nature of his own uncertainties. Hence narrative ambiguity, while not the only means of character subversion in the trilogy, is the central device by means of which that end is effected in all characters. Let us consider this ambiguity in each of the novels.

## *Volverás a Región*

On the simplest level, *Volverás a Región* appears to be a third-person narration framing a dialogue between two individuals who reminisce.[14] Specifically, the unnamed narrator at some unspecified time recounts a conversation between Doctor Sebastián and a woman, occurring sometime in the sixties. Their conversation, which deals primarily with events of the twenties and thirties, ends with the woman's departure. Soon after, the sound of a shot implies her murder. The narration ends with the murder of the doctor by someone apparently held captive in his house.

On the one hand, the fact that the fictive present begins with the arrival of the woman in a black car that day in the sixties indicates that the conversation between the doctor and the woman represents the primary focus of the work. But on the other, the narrator's intrusiveness and the nature of the dialogue itself provide evidence to undermine this interpretation.

First the intrusions. The narrator frequently interrupts his account of that evening in the sixties with lengthy digressions on three distinct topics. One, offered always in the present tense, is a minute description of the geological setting of the novel. Another set of digressions, also in the present tense, constitutes a series of aphorisms on the nature of human reality. "La conciencia y la realidad se compenetran entre sí: no se aíslan pero tampoco se identifican, incluso cuando una y otra no son sino costumbres" (p. 90). In the final set of intrusions, the narrator recounts, without character intervention, the events of the twenties and thirties directly: "Los primeros combates en la Sierra de Región tuvieron lugar a comienzos del otoño del año 1936, como consecuencia de los ataques llevados a cabo contra los pueblos de la vertiente oriental de la cordillera por unos pocos insurrectores de Macerta" (p. 31). The narrator himself, then, by the sheer quantity, length, and frequency of his obtrusive digressions, as well as by his apparent lack of concern for their relevance to the dialogue, contradicts the superficial evidence that the dialogue between the doctor and the woman is the primary focus of *Volverás a Región*. Indeed, he undercuts the very speakers he presents.

Secondly, such prevalence of dialogue raises certain expectations within the reader, expectations that are not met by the dialogue of the novel because, in fact, it shows few of the characteristics of dialogue. The numerous utterances, often exceeding five pages in length, are too long and incoherent to be retained, much less to invite responses. Change of speaker occurs without identities marked and without reaction by the other character. Lack of chronological order indicates that the content of those dialogues is not intended for communication. That is, by all indications, the quoted "dialogue" is not dialogue at all, but rather a series of interior monologues.[15]

Acceptance of the characters' "utterances" as unspoken expressions of the consciousness solves some problems but creates others. Given the presence of the narrator, we must first assume that the interior monologues are quoted. But the narrator repeatedly shows uncertainty as to the characters' thoughts: "Vaciló un instante y a la postre *pareció* adoptar la decisión a la que tanto se había resistido"

(p. 95, emphasis mine); and again, "*Parecía* decidido a no hablar más y a soslayer su presencia" (p. 100; emphasis mine).

The narrator's apparent lack of knowledge of the characters' thoughts converts the monologues from quoted to first-person, self-narrated monologues. Of this type of narration, critic Dorrit Cohn says:

> The kind and extent of the distance between subject and object, between narrating and the experiencing self, here also determines a whole range of possible styles and techniques . . . . To one side there is the enlightened and knowing narrator who elucidates his mental confusion of earlier days . . . . To the other side, there is a narrator who closely identifies with his past self, betraying no superior knowledge.[16]

She labels the former a dissonant, and the latter a consonant, narrator.

But neither term seems apt for the monologues of *Volverás a Región*. Certainly the narrating selves of the monologues exhibit aspects of dissonance as they look back on their experiencing selves. Yet their motives are inexplicable, the narrative aspects undercut by their stunning inability to elucidate or to organize that past in any way. Nor is the narrator in consonance with his former self, since he often refers to his present uncertainty. And finally, if the characters' utterances are in fact self-narrated monologues, what accounts for the presence of the narrator who speaks in the third person? What is his link to the doctor and the woman?

The intrusiveness of the narrator and the undermining of dialogue vitiate the value of the dialogue as oral interchange. At the same time, however, its ambiguity as self-narrated monologue is betrayed by the lack of purposeful direction within the resultant monologues. These factors point the reader to what appears to be a paradoxical novelistic structure: autonomous monologues concurrent with a more significant role assumed by the narrator. It is ultimately in forcing the reader's resolution of this apparent contradiction, as will become evident, that the ambiguity of *Volverás a Región* serves its fundamental purpose.

The monologues most closely approximate the autonomous variant that Cohn identifies as the "memory monologue."[17] In this type of monologue, the reader peers directly into a mind that focuses unconsciously on the past, with the present serving only as a spring-board to memories. Events follow not a chronological order, but one imposed by patterns of association.

But Benet's monologues, though apparently unspoken, are too consciously narrative to fall easily within this category. At the same time, we remember, the monologues are not orderly and purposeful enough to be self-narrated. The reader's inability to fit the mono-logues into conventional categories first clarifies their nature: the monologues are unspoken, conscious, disorderly, achronological, and unsuccessful analytical attempts to order the significance of the past. Next, the very existence of the monologues vitiates the dis-tinction presupposed by the two categories (self-narration, memory monologue), a distinction based on an opposition between reason and memory: when conscious, the mind's operations are governed by reason; when unconscious, memory prevails. The reader's in-ability to categorize these monologues challenges this opposition and, forcing the collapse of the two categories, affirms memory's primacy over reason: all of the mind's efforts to order the past—conscious as well as unconscious efforts—are controlled by mem-ory, rather than by logic or reason. The conscious mind works in much the same way as the unconscious mind: memory controls the mind, and not vice versa.

Reader inability to formulate characters in terms of paradigms, that is, to extract traits from their stories, focuses attention on the only fixed point of the novel: the moment of narration—the analyt-ical efforts of the mind—rather than on the past that is narrated. It is no coincidence, therefore, that the fragmentation of the novel's chronology does not affect the temporal sequence of the events oc-curring that night in the sixties.

"Characters," then, are presented as unmediated minds whose activity, opened to us directly, reveals the dominance of memory and disorder. They cannot be reduced to paradigms of traits be-cause, as their creation makes clear, the notion of such an orderly psychology is misguided in its disregard for the powerful role of memory.

If the minds of the characters are unmediated, does not this indi-cate a reduced, rather than increased, role for the narrator? The

narrator, initially appearing to be nonparticipating, calls attention
to himself by his intrusive reflections on the operations of his own
mind and on his own efforts to order reality. His becomes the unmediated mind of principal focus, jumping associatively rather than
rationally from subject to subject in efforts to order his own perceptions of reality, one that includes the existence of these characters.
His inability to know the characters' thoughts serves as a foil to the
reader's "privileged" position on the operations of those minds: the
human psyche, open or closed, is incomprehensible because by nature it is a chaotic montage of memories.

Thus while *Volverás a Región* initially appears to be a third person narration, its modulation toward a triple first person narration
is both medium and message: attempts to order human reality are
based on misplaced faith in reason. No perspective on human reality is more privileged than any other in offering the ability to order
that reality.

## Una meditación

*Una meditación* and *Un viaje de invierno* represent interesting, if
less complex variations on the ambiguity of the narrative stance
central to *Volverás a Región*. While the latter undermines conventional character by its reactions against the third-person/first-per-
son, reason/memory dichotomies to become a series of parallel autonomous monologues, *Una meditación* achieves a similar effect
via a different route, one to which the title itself points. Purporting
to be a first-person, retrospective self-narration, *Una meditación*
undercuts its self-narrative aspect and also modulates toward an autonomous memory monologue.[18]

The unnamed narrator, speaking in the first person, begins his account by establishing himself as what Cohn calls a dissonant narrator. A lucid narrating self, introduced here in the first sentence,
looks back on an experiencing self (that of childhood) introduced
in the second sentence:

De entre todas las quintas de la vega del Torce, al norte de Región, la de
mi abuelo, con ser de las más modestas, era una de las mejor emplazadas.
Apenas tenía otra tierra de labor que una huerta de unas dos hectáreas,
lindante con los viveros del río, definida y defendida por una cerca de

piedra a hueso por donde paseábamos de niños, como si se tratara de un camino de ronda, atentos a la pesca de ranas y la caza de sabandijas.[19]

Additional references on the same page to "mi abuelo" remind the reader of the narrator's involvement as experiencing self, while a doubt expressed by the narrating self ("no sé qué") reminds us of his control of the novel. That is to say, on the first page of *Una meditación* the narrator establishes himself, indirectly through the figure of his grandfather, as the axis of the novel. The narration of the following pages, which contain further references to incidents from the narrator's childhood, confirms this view. The expectations raised, therefore, are that the novel's meaning will lie in the progression of the narrator from ignorance to lucidity, in the ever-diminishing distance between the actions of the experiencing self and the reactions of the narrating self.

But two factors undercut the self-narrative aspects of *Una meditación*. As in *Volverás a Región*, one of these factors is fragmentation. The difference between the technique of the novels is instructive. In *Volverás a Región*, meaning emerges from the contrast between the fragmentation of chronology of narrated events and the chronological ordering of the narration itself. The former deflects reader focus from the novel's retrospective aspects (including conventional character development) while the latter simultaneously attracts it. Maintenance of some chronology is as structurally important to *Volverás a Región* as is the fragmentation against which it works. In *Una meditación*, the knowledge that time has passed is conveyed solely by the narrator's passage from childhood to adulthood, but the absence of any specific chronological frame of reference impedes a concurrent sense of character development. That is, in *Una meditación* the passage of time is empty; it carries with it no conventional concomitant character development.

The second factor undercutting the self-narrative aspects of *Una meditación* is the narrator's gradual disappearance as experiencing self. The end of the novel, which establishes its meaning through the experiencing self's progress toward greater lucidity, is particularly important in clarification and statement of the progress. Yet consider the final lines of *Una meditación*:

Apenas veía cuando llegó a la cerámica cuya fachada al principio no reconoció por la desaparición del barracón. Luego, adentrándose con temor, fue poco a poco pisando las cenizas que quedaban de él para caer de hinojos sobre el lugar que había ocupado su banco y restregarse la cara con la tierra negra, en busca de ese consuelo que sólo se encuentra en la desesperanza. (p. 329)

The narrator makes no reference to himself in this segment. In fact, the reader has no idea of whom he speaks, of his relationship to the character and events recounted, why he relates this incident, nor, significantly, why the novel ends here. The ending obfuscates rather than elucidates any process of development in the narrator, thereby undermining initial indications that meaning would lie in the narrator's growth in wisdom. If these factors serve to hinder the narrator's progress as experiencing self, several others draw attention to his narrating self. Most obvious of these is the graphic presentation of the novel. Three hundred twenty-nine pages long, *Una meditación* is presented without the logical divisions of paragraphs and chapters. Its physical being, then, supports the clue to its content given in the title: the novel represents the flow of one individual's thought processes, a meditation that follows the dictates not of reason and order, but of the chaotic associative forces of memory.

The narrator is strongly evident as processor of data in his transparent molding of his material: "*Quizá* la proximidad . . ." (p. 128; emphasis mine); "Hablo en términos generales, y no—aunque parezca mentira— . . ." ( p. 7). The innumerable sentences beginning with an elliptical *y* enhance the effect of subjective flow (pp. 117, 130, 138, 157, 160).

More important, however, the narrator of *Una meditación*, like that of *Volverás a Región*, calls attention to himself through his many intrusive interruptions of the narration, all of which in this case are musings on the nature of what he calls the "realidad psíquica" of the human being, the functioning of the *yo*. In his view, fear, "el estado general de la criatura para sobreponerse a un mundo hostil" dominates the psyche (p. 139). Reason, a tool used by the psyche to control fear, "se muestra incapaz de dar una explicación al destino" (p. 140). Reason's failure leaves the psyche defenseless in a hostile world, unable to know even itself.

Y cuando al azar el sentido de lo vivido quiere resumir para reconocer con datos objetivos un yo que le es imposible conocer . . . la continuidad se rompe con la aparición de un sujeto casi desconocido que al tiempo que desvela esa composición fragmentaria y caleidoscópica que escapa a su conciencia en un instante—un papel que cae, un aroma de la penumbra al cerrar una puerta, una mirada al reloj para constatar que las manecillas apenas han variado de posición, un número de horas que se aprestan a pasar por encima de los muebles, con su horrenda e hinchada mudez— comprende que la existencia puede no ser nada—ni siquiera el resumen— y, por ende, aquella pretendida justificación no es otra cosa que una añagaza para dar nombre a un no poder ser. (p. 65)

With the failure of reason the only means left the psyche to establish order is memory.[20]

sólo en el triste remedo de la memoria puede encontrar una mediocre satisfacción. Así es: se diría que es la memoria la tierra de nadie que sepa ambos modos del conocimiento [el de la conciencia, y el de la carne] y que ambos invaden en sus fútiles incursiones en busca del terreno del otro . . . . (p. 119)

Loosened from the artificial bonds of chronological time, memory remains, however ineffective, the sole means available for establishing order in human reality: "Sólo un vivir que haga desvanecerse al tiempo merece ser llamado así y todo lo que determina un presente acrónico—pasado y porvenir—no es mucho más que una abstracción a la que la conciencia le ha extraído su dimensión temporal" (p. 71).

The reader who seeks to order the retrospective aspects of the narration by imposing conventional structures of character progression through reason and chronology finds only obstructions in his path, and is ultimately redirected to consider the spontaneity— and futility—of the mind's analytical operations. By undermining retrospective aspects and the experiencing self while simultaneously directing attention to the narrating self, *Una meditación* becomes an extended variant of the autonomous monologue, focusing on what the mediative narrator himself calls "esa epifenomenal facultad del hombre de reflexionar sobre su propio pensamiento" (p. 94).

## Un viaje de invierno

*Un viaje de invierno* represents another level of refinement in the use of narrative ambiguity within the trilogy. As in the two earlier novels, reader expectations of conventional character development direct attention away from the narrator and narration itself, while structures within the novel direct attention to it. But whereas the earlier novels force resolution of the ambiguity, *Un viaje de invierno* demands that it endure.

From the conventional perspective, *Un viaje de invierno* appears to be essentially a third-person psychonarration directed by a consonant, nonparticipating narrator evident only in his sporadic marginal annotations, which, because they are unintelligible, are of uncertain relevance. Never openly referring to himself nor to his act of narration, the narrator primarily presents the obsessive thoughts (and some action) of two characters, Demetria and Arturo, about whom little information—and none of it in the form of a traditional plot—is divulged. Demetria, alone and unoccupied, plans a party to celebrate her daughter's impending visit. Arturo is a handyman who, apparently having previously worked on neighboring properties, has come now to work for her.

In his narration, the narrator never hints at his own opinions on the strange obsessions he relates. Thus, lines from the first paragraph on the writing of the invitations read as follows:

Las escribía siempre de su puño y letra, copiando en cada misiva un patrón redactado con anterioridad; pocas veces introducía el menor cambio entre una copia y otra y aunque con frecuencia su deseo le dictaba una cierta frase dedicada especialmente a un recipendario, a la postre su disciplina y su sentido de la equidad le forzaban a no salirse de la fórmula común para todos los invitados, relegando hasta su posible encuentro la expresión, de viva voz, de aquel sentimiento que le distinguiera del resto. Además había llegado a un punto en que le era forzoso preguntarse de qué valían tales distinciones: nada en su aprecio estaba más alto que el conjunto de circunstancias, casi todas comunes, que a cada uno empujaba a la comparecencia por lo que toda frase o gesto de bienvenida de índole particular tendría siempre un carácter ocioso.[21]

By detailing the temporal progression of Demetria's mental debate, the narrator absents himself from the narration, seeming to coincide perfectly with the thoughts he presents.[22]

On the other hand, if narratorial coincidence with the character serves to efface the narration, several other factors erode the novel's ostensible focus on the two characters. Most evident is the novel's extreme reduction of objective reality in the number of characters introduced, time elapsed, and action. In both *Volverás a Región* and *Una meditación*, allusion is made to baffling numbers of "characters," some of whom are even cited, whereas in *Un viaje de invierno* the narrator refers to only two other characters, and neither of them ever appears. The first two novels in the trilogy play upon the reader's expectations that repeated mention of a character implies plot significance, while the last does not.

Similarly, in *Un viaje de invierno* the time factor is reduced. The first two novels of the trilogy in one way or another allude to events occurring during the greater part of a lifetime. But in *Un viaje de invierno*, though infrequent reference is made to earlier years, temporal focus is primarily restricted to what seems to be a period of only several days.

Finally, as other critics have noted, *Un viaje de invierno* represents the further weakening of anything even remotely resembling traditional plot.[23] While the two earlier novels prod their readers into seeking a plot, promising, though never delivering, its emergence at every turn, *Un viaje de invierno* makes no such promises. Only one specific event (the party) is mentioned, and even then its actual occurrence is left uncertain. That is, while the reader conventionally looks to the objective reality of the characters for meaning, the diminishing of that reality in *Un viaje de invierno* is so severe that all attempts to order it are impeded.

Although the narrator of *Un viaje de invierno* appears to be in consonance with his characters, and thus much less evident than his counterpart in either *Volverás a Región* or *Una meditación*, in fact he frequently draws attention to his own act of narration. Self-revealing stylistic devices of editorial intervention and organization are used to this end:

Y aun cuando (*ella*) tenía para sí que (*él*) apenas conocía los números ni las letras, le constaba que sabía que se trataba de un calendario cuya utilidad . . . (p. 71, emphasis mine)

Era una idea que por su misma inverosimilitud cobraba . . . significación a la vista del manifiesto gusto del remitente por provocar su sorpresa, acaso derivado de su deseo de no dejarse nunca comer el terreno por sus (*los de él*) progresos en el arte de adivinar sus (*los de ella*) intenciones . . . (p. 76, emphasis mine)

. . . así la señora entendió que la complicidad de su sirviente en la convocatoria, preámbulo de la necesidad que de él tenía para el acontecimiento, sólo sería aceptable (*para él*) si de una u otra forma había de ser partícipe del doble beneficio . . . (p. 80, emphasis mine)

In all of the above examples, the narrator mockingly anticipates the doubts raised by his own narration, in effect stating his awareness of the doubts, yet refusing to restructure his writing to avoid them.

The abundant use of dashes and parentheses, even dashes within dashes and parentheses within parentheses, underscores the editorial participation of the speaker and thus indirectly asserts his presence (e.g., pp. 124, 111, respectively). Colons, too, generally infrequent punctuation in novels, are common in *Un viaje de invierno*, pointing up the narrator's organizational and explanatory concerns (e.g., pp. 157, 171, 175, 176). And in what is perhaps the supreme example of editorial self-revelation, the narrator utters a five-page sentence consisting of twenty-three parallel dependent clauses beginning with the word *que* (pp. 71–76). Similarly, the global perspective on time, as well as its fractionization, betrays narrative control: only a narrator can refer to a character's future life. Likewise, the statement that Demetria has reached the bottom step in her descent of a stairway, insignificant in itself, but particularly so when the reader has long since forgotten the beginning of the action, serves to expose the skeleton of the narration rather than to supply any useful information of the character herself (pp. 77, 146, 124, respectively).

On the one hand, then, psychonarration by a seemingly consonant narrator directs focus to Demetria and Arturo. On the other, the reduction of objective reality and the abundant evidence of the narrator's presence draw attention to the narrator himself. Where is the reader to look for meaning? How can the contradictory clues of *Un viaje de invierno* be reconciled?

Reconciliation is not possible; affirmation of this ambiguity is the novel's principal statement. Dorrit Cohn asserts that in psychonarration, "the stronger the authorial cast, the more emphatic the cognitive privilege of the narrator. And this cognitive privilege enables him to manifest dimensions of a fictional character that the latter is unwilling or unable to betray."[24] But the remarkable aspect of *Un viaje de invierno* is that the reader learns virtually nothing about its "protagonists." In the novel, that is, reader ignorance is an indication that the prominence of the narrator is not accompanied by the conventional cognitive privilege. The narrator, though highly visible, knows nothing. The irreconcilability of this ambiguity forces equalization of narrator and characters. *Volverás a Región* and *Una meditación* ultimately elevate the nonparticipating narrator to principal focus, but in *Un viaje de invierno* the ambiguity of focus merges narrator-characters into an indistinguishable collective human consciousness. Is it the narrator, or the characters, or both who repeatedly subvert reification of the *yo*? (pp. 99, 101, 143, 148, 198). Which of the three calls reason a dream? (p. 150). Which says that existence has no meaning, that education leads only to uncertainty? (pp. 155, 161, respectively). Whose perception is it that the concept of causality is worn out? (p. 165).

Isolated from speakers, all statements are equally attributable to character or to narrator.[25] The concept of coherent individuality is thus invalidated. The ambiguity in *Un viaje de invierno* intensifies and generalizes the statement of the previous two novels: human reality is incomprehensible from any and all perspectives:

> ese centro que dirige nuestros actos y que nos han acostumbrado a llamar voluntad o naturaleza o sociedad o conciencia ¿no será más bien el punto de convergencia y fusión de un continuo caótico que en el instante en que se concentra se asemeja . . . con un orden espiritual? Y si no quitamos la venda ¿no vendremos a reconocer que es el yo el verdadero impostor, aquel que sobre un orden anodino implanta la superchería de un caos al objeto de levantarse con la pretensión de edificar un segundo orden espiritual que impone su imperio y sus reglas sobre la tribal y patriarcal sociedad de la materia? (p. 198)

Reason is inadequate. Chaotic memory, "la más irresoluta de las potencias," dominates (p. 73).

Clearly, traditional character formation is inhibited in Benet's trilogy by means of several techniques. Essential among these is narrative ambiguity, through which the author invents characters marked by chaotic consciousness. As a result, they are irreducible to teleologically ordered paradigms of traits.[26] Conventional novelistic dynamics, dependent on oppositions established between at least two such paradigms, are in turn thwarted. Abandonment of futile attempts to make sense of the trilogy through structures based on such notions permits these new patterns to emerge. In this way, the reader is directed to the narration rather than to its object; to an analytical present rather than to a "meaningful" past; to the attempted conceptualization of narration rather than to a perceptual point of view within the story. The reader, that is, is directed to consider representation itself rather than the represented.[27]

Benet's rejection of established novelistic conventions presupposes new assumptions about human reality. In direct contrast to the readerly novel, Benet assumes the human psyche to be incoherent and unintelligible and reason to be an ineffective tool. He further suggests that no perspective on consciousness can alter this reality. Paradoxically rejecting conventional realism for a higher psychological realism, Benet directly refutes Forster's view that knowledge of characters' inner lives makes them more comprehensible and thus more human. Throughout, the trilogy discourse is designed to impede the emergence of character traits and not "to prompt their emergence."[28] Narrative ambiguity is thus a crucial literary element in the novels because it is largely through ambiguity that conventional character structures are undermined.

No vamos a ninguna parte, no olvidéis que fue la ambigüedad la que nos trajo aquí y si ahora nos queda sólo un camino no podemos olvidar que si aceptamos esta oferta fue en la seguridad de que todo da igual. (p. 126)

GONZALO DÍAZ-MIGOYO

# Reading/Writing Ironies in "En el estado"

Carmen:—¿Cómo podéis hablar de cosas que ignoráis?
El Sr. Arnau: -Precisamente.

JUAN BENET, *Un caso de conciencia*

The many difficulties of *En el estado* will not deter the faithful reader of Juan Benet who is, no doubt, already accustomed to Benet's brand of teasing narrative challenges and rewards. This time, however, the paradoxical nature of these challenges and rewards may surprise the reader: he will find that its uncharacteristically transparent prose leads into a blind alley, and once there, that the pleasure of reading is not based on avoiding the trap set for him but on falling into it. He may also remember that Benet had already tried something similar in his previous novels, particularly in *Un viaje de invierno* and *La otra casa de Mazón*.

*Un viaje de invierno* offered a double narrative in different keys: mythopoetic in the center of the page and rationalizing in the margins. Their relationship was one of substitution rather than of reciprocal explanation:[1] to accept the logic of the poetic narrative amounted to a dismissal of the marginalia's rationalizing thrust; and conversely, to insist on using the glosses as a guide to a rational understanding of the tale only succeeded in annihilating it. This narrative strategy repeatedly forced the reader to choose which road to follow: either the logical one or the mythical one. The priority of the latter was never in doubt, but to a large extent this assurance was due to the renewed confirmation that the marginal translations of the main text were unsatisfactory, although correct. The novel presented the reader with an insoluble problem, or

rather, it may be more accurate to say that it highlighted the insolubility of the interpretative quandary—even though, paradoxically,
it facilitated a strictly poetic reading of the text, because part of the
pleasure derived from the poetic narrative resulted from the impossibility of its logical translation.

In *La otra casa de Mazón*, Benet attempted something not altogether different. Here he tried a transvestism of comic and tragic
modes whose goal was, in Benet's own words, "an impossible
hybrid."[2] He attempted to escape the modal straitjacket that style
imposes on the subject matter not so much through a mere juxtaposition of both styles as through an exchange of their corre-
sponding masks. The chief similarity between this strategy and the
one used in *Un viaje de invierno* is centered in the notion of ironic
narrative attitude: ironic in *Un viaje de invierno* because of the
counterposing of its two mutually exclusive texts as if they were simultaneously affirmative and negative readings, and ironic in *La
otra casa de Mazón* because of the attempt to fuse the reciprocally
contradictory poles of style by means of disguises.

*En el estado* aims at something similar: the difficult operation of
revealing to the reader the inherent fiction of usual interpretative
attitudes. Benet invites the reader to view the spectacle of fiction at
work by forcing him to see himself reading—an operation fraught
with ironic reversals and reflections. This preeminent interest in
irony, however, should not be surprising in a writer who holds
opinions such as these:

> La literatura, la filosofía o la ciencia no son más que algo así como el
> disimulado acomodo del hombre al imperio del azar bajo la máscara del
> conocimiento. De esos acomodos hay uno que me interesa sobre todos y es
> aquél mediante el cual el hombre, al no saber cómo tratar de otra manera
> los problemas sobrenaturales que le circundan, se burla de un poder que en
> cualquier caso le domina. El recurso a la ironía.[3]

At first glance it would seem that Benet confuses here two types
of irony that we usually consider different: involuntary irony, that
is, irony of events, or objective irony, and intentional irony. But this
confusion is perfectly conscious. Actually, it is not even a confusion.
Objective irony is nothing but a tacit, willful irony in which the ob-

server, by attributing ironic intention to a fictitious supernatural agency, stubbornly maintains expectations that are contrary to the facts he witnesses. Intentional and objective irony are in fact the same basic type of mockery by the individual of a power stronger than he. In the case of the ironic novel, the writer himself is both an intentional ironist and a self-appointed observer, or describer, of objective ironies that he, of course, has created in the first place. The reader also plays a double role. He is as much a passive spectator of both types of irony as a secret ironist who maintains the validity of his own narrative beliefs and expectations by attributing ironic intention to the author of the narrative statements. There is plenty of evidence in *En el estado* to support this hypothesis, and some of it will be discussed later. First it may be helpful to sketch the general requirements of ironic statements so that the examples from the novel will be easier to understand.

A statement is ironic when the following three traits are noticeable: first, its prima facie verisimilitude. Without it the deceiving power is lost, since irony is based on an appearance of truth. Immediately thereafter the ironic statement must reveal itself as misleading. By taking the reader away from the original goal instead of toward it, it must reveal itself as contradictory. This is the second requirement of irony. Now, this contradiction may be due to an involuntary error on the part of the writer (or of the reader). Therefore, to understand that the statement is intentionally contradictory (ironic), the reader must be able to detect in it the trace of that intention; the trace of the writer's reason for endorsing that particular equivocality. We come thus to the third requirement of irony: given the circumstances of the ironist's utterance, the literal meaning of an ironic statement must refer to a desirable situation. Without the kind of circumstances that make the statement's literal meaning refer to a desirable, although inexistent or impossible, state of affairs, the reader cannot understand it as ironic.[4]

To what extent and with what consequences are these three conditions met in *En el estado*? The novel's verisimilitude, that is, its promise of traditional meaningfulness, is related to the apparent fulfillment of the expectations that it raises and encourages. *En el estado* creates them from the very beginning. Thus, the blurb in the book's cover reads: "Retomando el clásico tema de la relación que varios personajes hacen de sus vidas en el alto de un viaje . . . Juan Benet nos introduce en el mundo de tres lunáticos personajes, dos varones y una rancia dama, que narran . . . sus respectivos destinos y trayectorias."[5] It is immaterial whether these words are the publisher's or the author's. In either case they create the expectation of a traditional narrative development. Its fulfillment, though, is anything but traditional; so untraditional is it, in fact, that the original expectation has to be either discarded as impertinent or modified to the point of disfiguration. Even this decision is difficult to make. On the one hand, the irrelevance of the expectation is never completely obvious. On the other, it is not clear what its substitute should be. Consequently, the more misleading it turns out to be, the stronger is the reader's hope that it will eventually prove adequate.

The narrator keeps alive the reader's original expectation by extending a helping hand to him now and then. He rekindles hope with seemingly helpful allusions, but just as often the tale fails to fulfill their promise. Chapters I, II and III, for instance, seem to be firmly linked by the apparent clarity of the title of Chapter II: "Sucesos diversos que enlazan los precedentes con los siguientes" (p. 23). Yet in Chapter III the narrator immerses the reader in "Un tema de otro tiempo" where he begins, unaccountably, the story of the loss of the virginity of a mysterious old lady. Who is she, the reader wants to know. One of the travelers already introduced? With whom is she speaking? Where does the conversation take place? Nothing has been said about that.

Or take the recurring question, "¿ Circasiana?," with which the old lady's unknown interlocutor keeps interrupting her account. It insinuates insistently her relationship with the "acusados rasgos circasianos" (Chapter II) of La Señora Somer, one of the travelers. But the insinuation becomes immediately inoperative because at every turn the old lady rejects the question's relevance. Finally, she pronounces the word "circasiano" herself, and stops. Her puzzled interlocutor asks then "¿Qué pasa? ¿Por qué se detiene ahora?" and she explains: "En fin, me he equivocado una vez más, creía que era usted más perspicaz" (p. 43). The reader, able to recognize the word "circasiano" as a valuable clue, yet unable to determine what its value is, begins to see himself in the lady's interlocutor. He suspects that perhaps he is the one who lacks perspicacity—a suspicion that doesn't help his confusion.

The Spanish reader will find this question even more pointedly intriguing. It will remind him of some famous "pastillas circasianas" advertised in Spain a few years ago as a miraculous stimulant for breast development. He will, therefore, relate "circasiano" to the "senos pendulares" (p. 27) of the mad lady, so conspicuously mentioned in the previous chapter. Later on, he will remember the word again in this connection as he encounters yet another outrageous reference to this same woman's faded charms:

> con una alelada sonrisa hunde sus manos en el escote y extrae sus dos pechos que presenta al caballero como si se tratara de dos limones en manos de una frutera. "Por estos pechos, Ricardo, *mon roi.*"
> "Parecen calabacines," comenta Ricardo . . . "Y un poco pasados."
> (p.88)

Humorous allusions of this sort occur too often to list them all, but there is one exceptionally tantalizing type that deserves special mention: recognizable literary allusions. They come in all sorts: from the direct to the covert, not to mention outright parodies and pastiches—even of Benet's own idiosyncratic style. The intertextual quality of these passages satisfies, first of all, the literary vanity of the reader who is able to spot them. Taking advantage of that very satisfaction, the allusions make the reader believe that he should be able to find his bearings at the level of the model, since he is completely lost at the level of the narrative itself. But this orientation also proves impossible, even as it announces itself more and more insistently.

Consider, for instance, the repeated exclamation of that same old lady: "Oh, Richard, mon roi!" It makes one think of one of the British Richards: either the knightly Richard, the Lion Hearted, whose memory causes his damsel to sigh like that in Walter Scott's romances, or any of the Shakespearean Richards. The first connection is made possible by the abundant allusions to Brittany's knighthood to be found throughout the novel. The second is brought out by the end of Chapter XIV, the preposterous tale of the old lady's sixth orgasm, when one realizes that it is a potpourri of quotations from Cleopatra's death scene in Shakepeare's tragedy.[6]

These clues are so tempting, so obvious, so promising—even though it is not clear to what purpose—that I hesitate to point out only a few, instead of attempting to link all the loose ends of the puzzle. But ultimately I think that the reader must not allow himself to be thwarted by these obscure riddles. Instead, he must accept their teasing and deceitful nature and acknowledge that they lead nowhere but to their own interior, the interior of the fiction that they help create, rather than to any outside reality, literary or otherwise. And it is precisely by making this decision that the reader enters into the second phase of irony.

Before finishing the novel—which confirms that none of the stimuli achieve their goal—the reader already suspects that the contradictory character of the narrative is pervasive and intentional. He does not need to wait until page 204, near the end, where it is openly declared: "He aquí un último capítulo en el que, según es costumbre, se debería desentrañar el misterio. Pues bien, el que lo quiere descifrar es quien lo crea." The realization occurs much before that point, as soon as the reader notices that even the clearest of intimation is frustrating. For example, the description of Mr. Hervás on the second page: "Pequeño de estatura, tras haber disfrutado de un cuerpo macizo en sus años de plenitud ha adelgazado de manera tan desigual que al friso de su sexta década es contradictoriamente gordo y delgado, ancho y estrecho, consumido y lozano . . . . rasgos que en buena medida se corresponden con las notas más sobresalientes de su carácter."

Neither the narrator's admission of the contradictory nature of the character's appearance (or rather, of his own description of the character's appearance), nor the irony of the final assertion satisfies the reader's curiosity; instead, it spurs it on: "Surely Benet has a reason to admit this flagrant contradiction," thinks the reader. "No doubt, this will be cleared up later. I must keep it in mind as I read on." Of course, the day of reckoning never comes. After a few pages the reader is forced to abandon all hope, just as he has given up on organizing the action—or actions—chronologically, despite the repeated references in the text to temporal precedents and continuities. Some are obvious: "Recordará el esforzado lector que no bien se hubo detenido el autobús, el primero en pisar tierra de la Portada fue nuestro viejo conocido el señor Hervás" (p. 17). So is the already mentioned title to Chapter II: "Sucesos diversos que enlazan los precedentes con los siguientes" (p. 23). Others are more subtle and, as it were, apparently inadvertant, like the beginning of that same Chapter II: "Hervás vuelve de nuevo al campo despúes de su larga permanencia en la casa de las sombras" (p. 25). The reader has not been informed about that stay. He has, therefore, reason to be puzzled by the "de nuevo," to say nothing of the identity of "la casa de las sombras." He will be tempted, though, to assume that it is the same exit mentioned *later on*, in Chapter X, where it is pointed out that "el señor Hervás . . . sale de nuevo al campo en busca de Ricardo; y aprovecha el viaje para hacer una micción por la parte trasera del caserío" (p. 114).

One of the most effective ways in which the text frustrates the reader's curiosity—the very curiosity that it has excited before—is through the aforementioned literary allusions. The device is paradigmatic of all narrative inasmuch as it attempts to lead the reader to the point of departure, to fiction itself, to a referent whose reality is literary and, therefore, ultimately arbitrary and impossible to verify. All of the novel's characters—with the possible exception of its three theoretical protagonists—are taken from and refer to a world of fiction. Even their activities are nothing but a weaving of fictions. Take, for example, that Beckett-like couple, the innkeeper and his companion, called "El bulto." About the former we are told by way of introduction that "se dicen cosas muy graves. Se decían más bien años atrás" (p. 16). This is followed by a series of rumors each more outlandish than the last. About the latter we learn that he has come back from knightly Cornouailles by the Resporden of Concarnuea (we never know which) post. He then refuses to account for his travels and the innkeeper, in what he thinks is proper annoyance and just retribution, bites off one of his legs, reducing him to the "heap" he is now said to be. The reader may be here reminded both of the absurdities of Beckett (a favorite writer of

Benet) and of chivalric romances, but will not be able to make anything of these echoes.

The conversations of these two voices—it would be excessive to
call them characters—are just as recognizably allusive as their descriptions; and just as pointless. They deal, especially in Chapters V
and X, with the question of being and nonbeing, a subject in which
the reader hears echoes of among others, Calderón's "autos sacra-
mentales," Hegel and Heidegger, and even the writings of the Spanish counterculture guru, A. García Calvo.

In the case of the old lady, her family origins, rather than fictitious, are intentionally incredible. Her tale opens with the intriguing exclamation "¡Falacias, infundios!" (p. 37) only to culminate
with the last words of Shakespeare's Cleopatra: "Tell'st the world it
is not worth leave-taking" (p. 167). The subject on which she waxes
so eloquent is first the highly fantasized loss of her virginity and second her absurd desire to reach orgasm number seven without having to go through the drudgery of the sixth. Thus we have, so to
speak, two speculations on the subject of absence, or nonexistence.[7]

Consider the Prussian colonel Max Hoffman, bent on a new kind
of warfare: "Una contienda actual es una pugna entre dos previ-
siones que si están cuidadosamente desarrolladas, si se han consi-
derado los menores detalles, incluso aquellos reveses locales que
puedan amenazar la consecución del plan, apenas deben verse afec-
tados por los resultados en el campo" (p. 135). The whole thing has
a marked flavor, or is at least an inevitable reminder, of the best-
known military theoretician of modern times, Karl von Clausewitz.

All of these cases repeatedly stand out as theoretical, not practical; they are imaginary rather than concrete, and fictitious rather
than real. Inevitably, they frustrate any attempt at verification on
the part of the reader.

The most interesting of these figures is Pope Gapón. This outlandish personage is historical, although duly obscure and mysterious because of his covert activities at the turn of the century as a
spy for the Tzar's police in the Workers' Syndicate, and later in the
Social Revolutionary Party. Among other avatars equally fantastic
and improbable, he tells of his service in the household of Gustave
Flaubert. In his tale the novel offers its most representative passage,

one that I am tempted to call emblematic of the whole: the dealing with Flaubert's composition of his novella on the death of John the Baptist.

When the French writer began to describe the state of the sky at the beginning of our era, he came to doubt the accuracy of his astronomical knowledge and decided to ask a friend in Paris to check Arago's *Encyclopedie Astronomique.* As is well known, this incident really happened. But in the hands of Benet/Pope Gapón, it takes on a strangely fantastic aspect. Guided by "un aviso del más allá," Flaubert writes two sentences: ". . . la constelación de Perseo se hallaba en el zenit. Apenas asomaba Agalah . . ." (p. 188). Then, seized by the urge to verify this statement, he stops: he wishes to make sure that scientific knowledge agrees with imaginative intuition. He sets in motion thereby half of Europe's servants. And he does it, according to Benet, "con gesto zumbón y seguro de sí mismo (. . . con una anticipada ironía hacia todo el esfuerzo de Europa) . . . Toda la cultura europea, lo más granado de nuestra cultura—y no sólo los especialistas en astronomía, lenguas orientales o textos veterotestamentarios—se había de lanzar con verdadera pasión—y con exclusión de cualquier otro deber—al esclarecimiento de aquel enigma" (pp.192–93). This assertion is preceded by a dizzying list, in four dense pages, of fifty to sixty scholars, their works, their schools and relationships, a display reminiscent above all, of the false scholarship of Borges.

In commenting on the historical incident on another occasion Benet remarked that "un novelista desenfadado hubiera logrado un resultado casi equivalente [to the one that concerned Flaubert] si con un poco de desparpajo se hubiera decidido a violar las convenciones eruditas y adentrarse en los terrenos prohibidos de la fantasía."[8] It is Benet, though, who seems to have taken to heart this advice. He is the one who behaves like the novelist he fancied years ago, by pulling out of the hat that huge account of scholarly consultations. The ironic effect against Flaubert could thus have been perfectly achieved. But there is still one more loop in Benet's joke: it turns out that all those fifty or sixty names and all the works mentioned do correspond to real men and real texts, some alive and some well known at the time, 1877, in which Flaubert undertook the historical search. It turns out then that Benet has also taken Flaubertian pains to base his references on fact.

The irony that Benet once directed against Flaubert, as well as the irony that Flaubert is said to direct against that concerted European effort, has a boomerang effect for the reader of *En el estado*, both for the reader who assumes that Benet has brazenly invented those names, and for the reader, who, like Flaubert, has felt the need to verify their historical accuracy. In both cases the text proves that fiction refers only to itself even when it reflects a historical reality. It does so in this instance by means of two ironically contradictory examples: Flaubert's, in which fiction coincides with reality, and Benet's, in which reality seems fictional. All in all, this constitutes fiction's most definitive check on the reader's rationalizing urge: on the strength of his own behavior he is forced to admit that, like the supposedly passive observer of an objective irony, he—not Benet—has made this irony possible. He has done so by insisting on the use of rational expectations and probabilities as an obligatory counter to narrated fact. This conclusion is thus related to the third requirement of irony: the existence of narrative circumstances that make desirable, although impossible, the literal tenor of the ironic statement.

For whom could this type of novel, with such proliferating allusions, such obvious reliance on other literary texts, so openly exhibiting the problematic character of its interpretation, be desirable? No doubt primarily for a reader in hot pursuit of allusions, influences, and models; that is, for that intertextual reader who is so bent on tracing either facts or logical structures in fiction that he misunderstands its imaginative nature.

Benet himself may also find such a novel desirable, for by adopting the stance of the Socratic "eiron," he has feigned to accept all the opinions and expectations of this type of literary interlocutor, putting himself in the position to give his "esforzado" and "paciente" reader a revulsive dose of his own medicine—homeopathy with a vengeance. On Benet's part this is undoubtedly a question of revenge against a certain type of reader whom he finds particularly annoying. Benet's attitude toward and remarks about literary critics are sufficiently well known to make unnecessary here a repetition of his less than agreeable pronouncements on the subject.

I could conclude by pointing out that *En el estado* is a text whose only value is negative—a literary purge that tacitly cancels its positive virtues since, in catering and conforming to the taste of a certain kind of reader, it ends up proving its own irrelevance. That would be to adopt too narrow a perspective of this novel, however. Besides, when dealing with an ironic statement of novel length it is doubtful whether the normal negative consequences of all irony are pertinent.

Could it not be said that the type of reader mocked by Benet is the one who actually "creates" this irony? Doesn't he do so by imposing his own expectations and rationalizations on the "facts" presented by the novelist? Isn't the reader's anxious search for structure the real fiction here? And isn't the fiction of *En el estado*, then, the only undeniable fact at hand? It may well be, therefore, that the reader's attempt to attribute ironic intention exclusively to Benet is only a weak ploy to preserve the validity of his own traditional expectations, his own desired rationality.

I do not mean to imply that positive truth is wholly on the side of Benet, and false pretense on the reader's. Nor do I mean to reverse my preceding assertion that *En el estado* has only negative virtue. I mean, rather, that fiction seems neither more nor less fictitious than the reader's own rationality; likewise, that fiction, free from verifiable ties, is able to delight us in a real, although mysterious, way unavailable to rationality; and last, that ironic fiction seems the only way, paradoxically, to achieve a faithful and realistic depiction of reality—at least, reality when seen through the speculative prism so dear to Benet. Thus, it would be as valid a statement as any of the preceding to say that *En el estado* depicts the incoherence, the absurdity, the meaninglessness of existence, or, more pointedly, of certain concrete habits, opinions, individuals, and situations. But all this can only be partially true, just as it would be only partially true to describe the novel as a tour de force of literary slapstick.

The power of the ironic spiral is such that we cannot be its passive recipients or observers: if we do not ironize with the author of

*En el estado*, as often, as seriously, or as mockingly as he does, we cannot become his true interlocutors. We will merely be absurd fictional readers, as preposterous as the rest of the figures who parade through the novel.

DAVID K. HERZBERGER

# The Theme of Warring Brothers in "Saúl ante Samuel"

Unlike William Faulkner, with whom he is often compared, Juan Benet does not see the world as at once fallen and redeemed. On the contrary, Benet creates a fictional universe in which his characters are always crushed, always enveloped by the irremediable. They are denied redemption and thus condemned to despair, most frequently within a ruinous temporal flow from which they cannot hope to escape. This destructively tragic view appears throughout Benet's fiction, but inheres most pervasively in his early cycle of Región novels (*Volverás a Región*, 1967; *Una meditación*, 1970; *Un viaje de invierno*, 1972). It is not surprising, therefore, that *Saúl ante Samuel* (1980), which is set squarely within Región, should be informed by the same sense of fatalism.

More than any of his other novels, however, *Saúl ante Samuel* is impelled by a nihilistic historical perspective that focuses on the theme of warring brothers in the midst of the Spanish Civil War. To be sure, the war and its consequences have served as a backdrop for much of Benet's previous writing. In *Saúl ante Samuel*, though, the conflict moves to the fore as a crucial moment in history for an entire nation as well as for an individual family. The novel is thus "historical," in broad terms, as defined by G. R. Strange: "The serious historical novel . . . expresses a theory of history. Whatever its particular subject, it is designed to illustrate the necessary connections between the individual life and the social order, to arrive at a coherent interpretation of a significant moment of the past. In such a novel the main characters are often both individuals and representatives of historical tendencies."[1]

Benet draws clear parallels in *Saúl ante Samuel* between the Cain/Abel myth as it destroys a family and the broader destruction brought on by the Spanish Civil War. In contrast with more traditional historical novels, however, *Saúl ante Samuel* offers no clear political or ideological reasons for two brothers to choose opposing sides in the conflict. Instead, Benet suggests that the enigmatic forces of destiny have impelled their actions toward an inevitably ruinous fate. Similarly, Benet avoids portraying the Civil War as merely a battleground for two disparate ideologies. The political and social dilemma that gives impetus to the war scarcely surfaces in the narrative, and the fighting that takes place is empty of moral commitment. As a consequence, the novel emerges as a profound commentary on the tragic absurdities of the Civil War and, within this context, transforms the Cain/Abel myth in such a way that the concepts of punishment and justice become confounded and ambiguous.

As in much of Benet's earlier fiction, the plot of *Saúl ante Samuel* defies synthesis. For the most part, however, the narrative revolves around the personal conflict between Martín and his older brother on the one hand, and the battle for Región between the Republican and Nationalist military forces on the other. Throughout much of the novel the actions of Martín determine the principal course of events. After moving away from the family home near Región to pursue a career in the capital, he is called home by his father after the Republican militia detains his brother in August of 1936. The family's political views ally it closely with the Nationalist movement, but Martín has dissociated himself from family tradition and is considered a radical by many friends and relatives. Following Martín's return to Región his father orders him to join the Republican forces in order to help his brother escape death at the hands of Republicans. After two years Martín becomes a commander in the Republican army and participates in combat against the Nationalists in the mountains of Región. His brother is eventually killed, however, and Martín's actions in the incident contribute directly to his death. The two principal plot lines (sibling rivalry and the Civil

War), therefore, are intimately linked throughout the narrative and sustain a sense of irremediable ruination that makes *Saúl ante Samuel* the most destructively pessimistic of all of Benet's novels.

The Civil War has appeared as a secondary thematic concern in much of Benet's previous fiction. For the most part, Benet portrays the war and its aftermath as a pernicious blight that corrodes the very soul of society. Spain thus exists as a decrepit organism on the verge of spiritual and physical dissolution. In *Volverás a Región*, for example, the novel in which the Civil War is portrayed with greatest immediacy, a vision emerges of a violent and senseless conflict that separates two periods of destruction: a prewar society torn by chaotic discord, a postwar society crippled by decay. In *Una meditación*, Benet addresses a more specific aspect of the fighting—the desire for not only victory, but for complete annihilation of the enemy. Rather than pursue constructive reconciliation after the war, the Nationalist victors (in Benet's view) sought only to broaden further the schism between the two sides:

> . . . un ánimo inquieto, vengativo y malévolo prevalecía en todos los triunfadores que todos los días, a todas las horas y en todas las esquinas alardeaban de su victoria para lo que no era suficiente glorificar su gesta sino que necesitaban cubrir de insultos a su adversario como si recelosos e inseguros de su triunfo sin decidirse a bajar la guardia y dispuestos a enarbolar en todo momento las banderas, las razones, las armas y los principios que les movieron a la lucha, necesitaran todavía mantener la contienda con la palabra, ese recurso final cuando la acción es impotente, y una estela de rencor, menosprecio y cierta indiferencia que dejó el barco que se llevó a todos los derrotados, ansiosos de tener entre sí y sus hermanos un océano cuando menos.[2]

Although Benet lays blame for postwar stagnation squarely on the shoulders of the Franco regime and has little sympathy for forty years of oppression, he also conveys in his fiction a certain ambivalence toward the Republic.[3] He hints at the divisiveness of prewar society and, when focusing on the war itself, he ridicules the Republicans' military strategies and assails the general disorder of their armies. In fact, much of the fighting portrayed in his narrative borders on the absurd, though the death and despair associated with it remind us of the war's constant horror. Beyond this, however, Benet's portrayal of the Civil War is rooted in a profound skepticism toward historical Manichaeism. That is to say, he dipicts the war in a way that deprives it of ideological substance. In none of his novels does he seek to define the conflict as good against evil, or right versus wrong, but rather frames the war in ambiguity. The immediacy of battle always supersedes political conflict in Benet's narrative, and the moral imperative of social justice recedes into obscurity as the energies of destruction move to the fore. It is for this reason that *Saúl ante Samuel* stands as his most important statement (in his fiction, at least) on the war, since it adumbrates his perception of moral ambiguity on a mythic scale. The novel carries on a broad intertextual dialogue with much of his previous narrative, but the major focus clearly underscores the theme of warring brothers—not only within a family, but also in a tiny, isolated area (Región), and the whole of the nation.

Much of the description of the Civil War in *Saúl ante Samuel* focuses on the military strategy involved in the struggle—ultimately won by the Nationalists—for Región. Similar to his depiction of the war in *Volverás a Región*, Benet details the battle plans of the Republican and Nationalist armies as if writing a military manual. His style is lean and direct, and the battle vividly takes shape before the reader's eyes. In contrast to *Volverás a Región*, however, Benet undermines much of the military strategy (especially of the Republicans) at the same time that he seeks to explain it through the interpolation of editorial commentary. Thus, for example, when describing the Republican offensive he interjects "si así se puede dominar;" or "se permiten el lujo de confiar en el entusiasmo."[4] Benet's criticism of the Republican hierarchy of command is even more explicit. Only when defeat in Región seems certain does the Republican Defense Committee cede its power to the professional soldiers. As the head of the committee admits to Martín:

Convencidos de la justicia de nuestra causa hemos confiado en exceso en el peso de una historia que por encima de los acontecimientos diarios terminaría por establecer el resultado final a nuestro favor. . . .Es lo malo de contar con una visión profética pues en el fondo hemos sido nosotros los que hemos confiado en la providencia, los que hemos apelado a los objetos sagrados de nuestro siglo, los que hemos rezado, invocado y sacrificado a

los dioses modernos en tanto nuestros enemigos se armaban. . . . Hemos
sido los únicos creyentes en una fuerza invencible. . . . y así nos ha ido.
(p. 347)

In short, the military aspects of the Civil War in Región come
clearly into focus, and Benet reiterates his belief that the war was
shaped by a zealous commitment to nihilism: "El deseo de destruir
no solamente haciendo uso de los medios materiales y de las armas,
sino también por el espíritu; de aniquilar otras ideas, frustrar otras
aspiraciones y condenar otros paraísos" (p. 56).
The Civil War influences life in Región in other ways as well.
During the war everything became contingent upon the nature of
the fighting in the present, or upon one's perceptions of the eventual outcome in the future. Thus Martín's family and relatives seek
shelter in the large family home and wait for events to take their
course. Yet waiting always coincides with stagnation in Benet's fiction, and inaction inevitably leads to decay. Hence Martín's father
sits "tembloroso en un rincón, con la manta sobre las piernas, las
manos sobre las rodillas y la cabeza incapaz de refrenar su agita-
ción, con la mirada clavada en esa puerta a la espera de que entre
quien ya no le puede sacar del miedo que tiene a morir" (p. 125).
Similarly, Martín's brother remains in hiding for much of the war,
and he appears as "[un] héroe que se pudría en una habitación mi-
serable" (p. 327). The family house itself becomes a central image of
sterility and decadence as it exists amid silence and shadows, and
eventually its rotting shell serves as a vivid reification of the physical and spiritual dissolution caused by the war.
The pervasive destructiveness of the Civil War, the absence of
ideological rigor, and Benet's ambivalent explanation of the fighting
can be explicitly linked to the conflict between Martín and his
brother (that is, the Cain/Abel myth) in several important ways.
First of all, the national fratricide of the war is echoed on a more
personal level by the antagonism between the two brothers. This
conflict emerges concretely through their identification with opposing sides of the fighting and has implicitly vitiated their relationship
for decades. Furthermore, since Martín serves as a commander in
the Republican army, the nature of his continued ambivalence toward his brother's dilemma (as a prisoner of the Republicans) par-

allels that of the Republican uncertainties about how to deal with the Nationalists. In addition, the same ambiguous morality that characterizes Benet's perceptions of the war as a whole marks his portrayal of the personal battle between Martín and his brother. Above all, however, the fate of the two brothers depends to a large degree upon the course of the Civil War. Although their personal conflict stems from the early days of their youth, it is during the war itself when their long-time strife must finally be resolved. Every aspect of their own existence, as well as their relations with others, is conditioned by the Civil War that surrounds them. And as if to echo the path of the fighting in Región their conflict must also end in a nihilism in which ideological commitment plays no part. As will be discussed, however, Benet confounds the dilemma of the two brothers by denying them the freedom of choice at the very moment when they seek to forge their own destinies. Indeed, the future is more closely tied to their *abuela*'s mysterious cards than to their own free will, and the destiny that awaits them coincides with the same tragic destruction that marks the outcome of the Civil War.

Benet's version of the Cain/Abel myth is in many ways a historical narration (that is, the history of the family, as it is in the Bible), though his vision of the myth as irredemptive tragedy clearly distinguishes it from the biblical account.[5] In the first place, although Martín and his brother share the same mother, the narrator strongly suggests that Martín was fathered out of wedlock by his mother's lover. Hence Martín is born into a climate of suspicion and antagonism, while his brother enjoyed the favored status of legitimacy and primogeniture. Furthermore, Martín's mother died a short time after his birth, and Martín was left to struggle with a father who rejected him and a brother who tried to escape his company. In fact, Martín's brother, though he ultimately comes to be identified with the mythic figure of Abel, hardly incarnates the innocence and piety through which the traditional Abel wins redemption. Indeed, Benet nurtures a view of him throughout the narrative that vitiates the esteem and grace shown him by his father. For example, he treats his cousin (one of the principal narrators) "no de tú a tú, ni de primo a primo, ni de niño a chico, sino de superior a inferior, de rico a pobre, de hijo a orfelino y de dueño a inquilino menesteroso"

(p. 178). In addition, he carries himself with an air of superiority that stands antithetically opposed to the humility of the traditional Abel: "Su hermano formaba parte de la legión que no hace públicos los errores propios y no sabe comportarse sino como superior al que tiene delante" (p. 306). Hence Benet's Abel—he is referred to ironically as "piadoso Abel" (p. 132)—emerges as a near demonic character who appropriates the paternal affection due his brother and who consistently disparages his fellow beings.

For his part, Martín never succeeds in integrating himself into the womb of his family. As a child he must endure the aloofness of his brother and bear the stigma of his mother's adultery. Thus as an adult he seeks to escape his family by fleeing to the capital. Although he leaves Región with a profound sense of hatred, he harbors only vague notions of revenge. What is important about Martín's flight to the capital, however, is that it represents an urgent quest for identity. It is as if he senses the mythic patterns of destruction that are forming about him and desperately strives to forge his destiny outside these patterns. Hence his only apparent salvation in order to live with himself is to repudiate his family (that is, his past) and move beyond their reach. His escape is suddenly and irremediably cut short, however, by the outbreak of the Civil War and the appeal from his father to return home to help his brother. The very act of returning represents a supreme sacrifice for Martín (that of freedom to design his own future), but there is no indication that he will be rewarded for this sacrifice. Indeed, nothing in the narrative suggests that if he saves his brother he will be welcomed as the prodigal son. Furthermore, his return places him in the midst of the Civil War, which underscores the parallel development of his own conflict with that of the war in Región.

At first glance it may appear that Martín is meant to symbolize the wronged brother; that he has been victimized by fate and has responded rationally, even nobly, to his predicament. His emergence as a Cain figure in Benet's mythic construction, therefore, would seem to lack the necessary substance to make it ring true. However, as discussed earlier, there is no Manichaean notion of good and evil in Benet's narrative world. Hence, like his brother, Martín too falls from grace. Before his return home the opportunity for revenge against his brother presents itself unexpectedly. His brother's wife, mistreated in much the same way as Martín, entices Martín into incestuous adultery as a means of punishing her husband. Thus when the telegram arrives from his father ordering him to return home, Martín does so with profoundly ambivalent desires. Until now he has not actively sought to destroy his brother and has certainly not considered murdering him. Driven by desire for his sister-in-law, however, he begins to contemplate a final act of revenge that would lead to his brother's death. He accedes to his father's will and joins the Republican army, but at the same time is impelled toward fratricide by the incestuous longing for his brother's wife. Benet clearly conjoins the thematic centers of his novel most intimately at this point in the narrative, for the two brothers are at war on both a personal and historical level: one a Nationalist, the other a Republican; each in conflict with a brother of his own blood. And just as both sides of the Civil War are concerned only with winning the battle at hand, yet cannot hope for redemption through victory, so too the two brothers pursue a fratricidal war in which only tragedy can prevail.

The interweaving of fragments describing the Civil War with those depicting the conflict between Martín and his brother recurs throughout the novel in a variety of circumstances. The coincidence of the two themes is articulated most succinctly by the *abuela* in one of her soliloquy-like dialogues with Martín: "Sobre el esplendor de nuestra tierra y sobre la dicha de nuestra tierra se cierne una época de ruina" (p. 135). This fatalistic conception of a ruinous destiny, both for the family and Región as a whole, clearly affirms the principal narrative focus on the theme of warring brothers. Furthermore, it links *Saúl ante Samuel* to Benet's previous cycle of Región novels. The inhabitants of Región repeatedly succumb to decadence and despair, and their only legacy from history is solitude and isolation. The *abuela*'s power to foresee the future through the reading of her cards also suggests a link with Benet's earlier fiction and his cultivation of the enigmatic. On several occasions, in fact, the cards supersede the *abuela*'s physical presence and become a metonymic device that conveys the sense of inevitable tragedy awaiting both the brothers and the nation as a whole. The *abuela*'s age ("se extingue pero no se muere" [p. 142]), her power over the

other inhabitants of the house ("Abría resueltamente los ojos [y] no
sólo su cara quedaba trasmutada sino que un cambio se producía en
toda su persona, en la alcoba, en todo el ámbito alrededor de ella,
incluso en toda la casa y sus contornos que parecían apaciguarse
bajo su mirada" [p. 23]), and her philosophical ramblings on the
destiny of the family are all tied to her powers of divination and, by
extension, to Benet's exploration of enigma.

Beyond her ties to the enigmatic, however, the *abuela* continu-
ously serves to enhance theme. She narrates much of the conflict between the two brothers and associates it with the broader struggle
of the Civil War. She articulates as well the manner in which Benet
metamorphoses the traditional myth of Cane and Abel through his
blurring of the distinction between good and evil: "Parece que el
bien y el mal distan tan poco el uno del otro, que son como dos
líneas concurrentes, que aunque parten de apartados y diferentes
principios, acaban en un punto" (p. 56). In short, in her role as narrator she intensifies the sense of doom and decay that weighs upon
the family in the present, and foresees a tragic dissolution in the
future through the act of fratricide.

Although rivals since their youth, the two brothers are drawn to
opposing sides of the Civil War in a fortuitous sort of way. While
Martín's brother chooses the tradition of privilege and money
through his support of the Nationalists, Martín at first opts for indifference. In a paradoxical twist that marks Benet's penchant for
defamiliarizing plots and themes, Martín becomes a Republican at
the request of his father (as discussed earlier) and thus goes to war
with his brother in order, ironically, to save him. The Cain/Abel
myth clearly grows convoluted here, for Cain (Martín) is asked to
rescue his brother rather than murder him at the same time that he
commits adultery with his brother's wife. The traditional motivation for vengeance, therefore, as well as the notion of salvation for
the innocent, is turned upside down. Indeed, innocence does not exist in Benet's mythic world, hence both brothers fall into irredemptive sin.

The final resolution to their conflict is ambiguous in its plotting,
but direct and concise in its message. Martín's brother is indeed
murdered, but Martín is not the murderer. He could have prevented

the killing, but chose to deceive his brother and allow him to try to escape from his hideout even though his life was in danger. Thus Martín is implicated in his brother's death but remains exempt from total guilt. Clearly, Benet alters the parameters of the Cain/Abel tale within the framework of the Civil War in order to suggest an ambiguous resolution to an eternal, mythic problem. For Abel is not really Abel in Benet's myth, just as Cain is not really Cain. Instead, each is transfigured into the other, and all that remains for them is death, decay, and exile—the only true heritage of the fratricidal conflicts that take place in Región.

What finally subverts the traditional constructs of the myth in *Saúl ante Samuel,* however, what prevents it from becoming a modern-day morality tale, is the pervasive and destructive power of fate. For Benet, like Faulkner and Proust before him, man is not condemned to be free in an existential sense, even though he suffers the anguish of living in a world without meaning. Instead, Benet's characters are condemned even before they can make a choice. They are ruled by fate, "esa dispersión de tu materia en partículas que aparentemente unidas en torno a ti bailan en secreto al compás de un ritmo inaprensible" (p. 256). The concept here of existential despair lying beyond the control of the individual links *Saúl ante Samuel* to much of Benet's previous fiction, as well as to his preoccupation with the mysterious and enigmatic. More important in the present context, however, it undermines the concept of a divinely ordered universe, which in turn suggests a chaotic world where justice—the ultimate moral legacy of the Cain/Abel myth—is a chimera. Furthermore, as the *abuela* explains to Martín: "Los actos de los hombres no son de ayer ni de hoy y ni siquiera les pertenecen. Y la voluntad de hacerlos ¿no es el juguete de un designio que jamás llegarán a comprender?" (p. 106). The notion of time here is crucial, for it places man outside a temporal flow that is measured by traditional perceptions of present and past. This temporal obscurity contributes to the chaos of man's vision and, in relation to the theme of warring brothers, destroys the power of myth (that is, it obliterates time, and therefore, history) to serve as a paradigm for human conduct.

There is much in *Saúl ante Samuel* that brings to mind Benet's

earlier cycle of Región novels: the customary peripatetic style, a
fragmented temporal flow, the conflict between reason and instinct,
a sustained ambiguity. Yet more than any of his previous novels,
*Saúl ante Samuel* offers a vision of irredemptive tragedy on a historical and mythic scale. This is not to say that Benet proposes moral-
istic dogma or that he has written a thesis novel with a singular,
canonical perspective. Instead, he appropriates the myth of Cain
and Abel and transforms its traditional clarity of message into a
pall of equivocal abstruseness. The Civil War does not appear as a
battle between right and wrong; thus the nobility of its cause is first
confounded, then vitiated by a profound sense of nihilism. Similarly, the conflict between Martín and his brother cannot be nar-
rowly defined by traditional mythic patterns with a dualistic view
of what is just and what is not. For there are no absolute values in
Benet's world, no affirmation of the wholly good or wholly evil. Indeed, the only truth that stands infallible is that man's fall into despair cannot be prevented. The fratricidal war (both between brothers and the forces of a nation) that takes place in Región, therefore,
may solve the immediate question of who shall live and who shall
die, but cannot bring redemption to the victor.

RANDOLPH D. POPE

# Benet, Faulkner, and Bergson's Memory

In his essay "De Canudos a Macondo," Juan Benet tells the story how, in the spring of 1945, he was in a bookstore on the street of San Bernardo searching for a text by Fabre.[1] He made a clumsy movement that threw open to the floor a book in a nearby bookcase. One of the pages of the book, he remembers, said nothing more than:

VARDAMAN

My mother is a fish

He had just stumbled upon William Faulkner. This accidental discovery represents a crucial moment in Benet's literary career. He has frequently affirmed that Faulkner's influence was decisive in his writing, and many critics who have studied Benet's works consider this influence evident. But the matter is complex and merits reexamination and expansion, however brief, in order to open possible avenues of further investigation.[2]

From the beginning we are faced with a dilemma, since the question of influences, even when avowed by an author, falls outside the scope of the central preoccupations of today's critical thought. On the one hand, the characteristic traits of a text are not considered as the intellectual property of an individual; on the contrary, they are seen to surpass him or her and are attributed to a variety of factors, such as archeological stratum (Foucault), period (Rama: *Rubén Darío*), horizons (Jauss), and strategies of reading (Culler). On the other hand, the writer is trapped amid a paradoxical mix of societal

forces: the desire for innovation and original thinking, countered
by the reductive demands of a one-dimensional, mass society. The
writer may seek to engage the attention of the reader through the
shock of novelty or complicated technical strategies, but often a text
plagued by difficulty deters the very readers for which novelty has
been intended. At the same time, the mere hint of influence in the
writer's quest for difference often results in an anxiety (Bloom) or a
burden (Bate). A scandal ensued when Manuel Pedro González suggested that Cortázar was at least part of a long tradition, if not de-
rivative. Furthermore, to blind ourselves to influences helps to
avoid facing the serious obstacles now confronting the writing of a
history of literature, a genre that seems to be passing away to the
dismay of some. Many critics today prefer a collection of articles
(such as the present volume), or descriptions of literature in historical texts (as proposed by Raymond Williams) to the traditional
writing of literary history. Even sociologists of literature like Erich
Koehler are forced to acknowledge that literary change is often best
explained as exclusively pertaining to a discrete realm, literature.[3]

Further complicating the matter is the fact that Benet appears initially as an isolated specimen in the gamut of Spanish postwar literature. But later, at the moment of success and recognition, he is
joined by other writers—the preceded, as Borges would say—
among whom one of the most important is Luis Goytisolo.[4]

Yet once one takes up the question of influences—and not of in-
tertextuality or resonances, two clever ways of sidetracking the
question—one detects that Faulkner's influence on Benet has been
analyzed up to now primarily at a level that includes coincidences
of topics and strategies.[5] Let us examine briefly some of these points
of contact, and consider if they are peculiar to Benet:

(1) The creation, mapping, and populating of a fictitious region
that is perceived as a microcosm of historical reality and is perme-
ated by typical, recognizable elements that refer to that historical
world. As Benet puts it, this region is "un paradigma en escala
menor."[6] Macondo, Región, and the somber world of Onetti all fall
under this heading. Even if, strictly speaking, to create such a world
is by no means a novelty introduced by Faulkner, it is quite evi-

dent that his example is determinant for the writers that I have mentioned.

(2) The crucial importance of mythical or biblical references as a guide to the reading of a text or as submerged paradigm (Numa and Demeter in Benet, the Wandering Jew in García Márquez). Some of the titles of Benet's novels reveal this trait: *El ángel del Señor abandona a Tobías* (Barcelona: La Gaya Ciencia, 1976), and *Saúl ante Samuel* (Barcelona: La Gaya Ciencia, 1980). Benet has also written a superb analysis of the style of the Old Testament.[7]

(3) The investigation of subjectivity, that takes place in long, complex, and rambling sentences (one can also think of Roa Bastos or Carpentier), and the counterpoint of different versions and voices (as found in *As I Lay Dying*), that are often more contradictory than complementary. Faulkner explained in an interview: "I think that no one individual can look at truth."[8]

(4) The central role of civil war, American, Spanish, Colombian, Mexican, Paraguayan, respectively for Faulkner, Benet, García Márquez, Carlos Fuentes, and Roa Bastos.

All of these coincidences and relationships seem arbitrary and almost incoherent. In the case of the Latin American novelists, they reveal a fragmented utilization (even creative plundering and misreading) of elements convenient for projects that are also grounded in many other traditions (Pre-columbian, cinematic language, Marxism, *criollismo*, and so forth). In contrast, while Benet confesses that other authors have left an imprint on his writing, such as Melville, Conrad, Kafka, Proust, Thomas Mann, and Rilke, there is in him a peculiar proximity to Faulkner that sets him apart from the other writers previously mentioned. This affinity is seen as deeper when one realizes that both writers use as integral parts of their narration a whole set of theoretic postulates that explain the main narration and sometimes become a coprotagonist, much as a Greek chorus. It is here that I believe one should explore the affinities between both novelists. In Benet, as in Faulkner, one finds frequent meditations on the value of time, action, and memory, and further considerations about a world that resists human will until the latter is defeated (not by reasons that are externalized, such as the power of the jungle or of a dictator as in the Latin American novels, but by metaphysical reasons).[9]

Benet and Faulkner find the origin of their formulations and questions in the common fascination that both declare to have felt for Bergson's philosophy.[10] The main points in Bergson's work that become central in the narrative world of Faulkner and Benet are the following:

(1) Perception is never pure, but instead comes into being under the weight of the whole of memory. The past, according to Bergson, "all of it, without a doubt, follows us in every instant."[11] In another book he writes: "There is no perception that is not impregnated by memory." And he adds: "To perceive becomes only an opportunity for remembering."[12] For Benet "la memoria mantiene abierta la cuenta;"[13] and for Faulkner "Maybe nothing ever happens once and is finished."[14] Most of Benet's characters, as many of Faulkner's, constantly labor with phantoms of the past fed by a relentless memory. At an anecdotal level, a series of phantoms roams the works of Benet, from stories like "TLB" to *Una tumba*, or meditations about the myths of phantom ships. At a deeper level, every sentence is haunted by disquieting ghosts that give to Benet's texts the density of a palimpsest. To see clearly and directly into reality this obsessive memory must be penetrated, more a longing of nostalgic memory than a true possibility. "La paz del prerreflexivo" hinted at in *Un viaje de invierno* is always misplaced somewhere beyond the present situation.[15]

(2) Scientific time is not human time, since the latter is determined by consciousness in the elastic duration of instants that have their own peculiar density (one remembers Borges's "El milagro secreto"). In Faulkner's and in Benet's novels there are clocks that contradict each other or characters who encyst themselves in a moment that anchors them in what for everyone else is the past. In the Princeton room of *The Sound and the Fury* menacing clocks mark time for suicide, while in Benet's *Una meditación* the starting up of the clock with which Cayetano Corral has tinkered for seemingly endless, timeless years presides over the destruction of the youthful characters. In *Absalom, Absalom*, Miss Rosa Coldfield declares: "My life was destined to end on an afternoon in April forty-three

years ago," [16] just as in Benet's first important novel the memory of the child is fixed on the instant at which he was abandoned by his mother. In this same novel, one reads: "el tiempo no puede existir" (*Volverás*, p. 281), while Faulkner affirms: "There isn't any time. In fact I agree pretty much with Bergson's theory of the fluidity of time. There is only the present moment, in which I include both the past and the future, and that is eternity." [17]

(3) History moves (not necessarily progresses) because of the impulse of vital energy. This energy is not inexhaustible, and it must struggle against the resistance offered by the body and the inertia of all matter. (In relation to this, it is interesting to note how often Benet refers to the soul.) The worst, for Benet, is "una sociedad agotada" (*Volverás*, p. 17). For Faulkner, in *The Sound and the Fury*, each of the Compson brothers possess creative energy that stagnates and annihilates itself. [18]

(4) To express the experience of a heterogeneous and fluid reality the human being must use a language that by nature is discontinuous and homogeneous. Abstraction itself petrifies the flow of life, and generalization casts the diversity of beings under one blanketing label. [19] No state begins or ends, as sentences do, but instead they all mesh one into another. [20] In an essay about the craft of writing, Benet observes that one does not pay attention to the fact itself, but goes back to its antecedents and insinuates its consequences. [21] In *Absalom, Absalom*, Faulkner declares: "living is one constant and perpetual instant" (p. 142). Using all of memory one can bore again and again into an instant until reaching the deepest level in which all of its implications are revealed. [22] Until this task is accomplished, Benet's characters will feel uneasiness, insecurity, uncertainty and will perceive around them enigmas and secrets of unceasing ambiguity. Most of Benet's characters experience an epiphany in which all of their past becomes present—or makes itself present: "el día en que se produce esa inexplicable e involuntaria emersión del recuerdo" (*Una meditación*, p. 31). The reader must also come to terms with the avalanche of disjointed material that the narrator offers and experience a feeling of completion when all of memory makes sense. Unfortunately, these fleeting moments of insight are burdened by the knowledge that not all enigmas are resolved for the

characters or for the readers. But in the effort to figure out existence as a totality, sentences reflect the complexity of the mind's path where diverse moments of time come together, opening up to discovery a constellation of forces buried in the past and actively determining the coordinates of future action. In this sense, a world saturated by ruins (and runes), such as the one favored by Benet's narrations, is predominantly seen as historical, as a time of past splendor, now removed from and missed by the nostalgic imagination, but also dangerously exerting its power, sometimes in a senseless obedience to commands given in altogether different circumstances that may even have been forgotten. The sequence of the multiplicity of instants points always, in Faulkner as in Benet, to a tragic consequence—murder, suicide, rejection—and that is why scrutinizing the tangle of the past/present is so urgent.

The desire to transcend the abstraction of language leads to an accumulation of qualifiers, shades of meaning, and to the reiteration of slightly modulated statements. ("Cumulus" is one of the words used most often by Benet.) This longing to trap the complexity of a lived reality also leads to the search for a slow rhythm, in which the pulse is marked by riddles and allusions that impart in their failed grasping that "what really occurred" is never delimited by the narrative voices. This is related to Benet's belief in the "radical insuficiencia del conocimiento" (*En ciernes*, p. 34) and to the fact that "es inteligible el ímpetu de vivir" (*Viaje*, p. 95). Therefore, literature, according to Benet, has as a mission to "demostrar la insuficiencia gnoseológica" and must aim to "fomentar la invención de aquella clase de misterio que por su naturaleza se encuentra y se encontrará siempre más allá del poder del conocimiento" (*En ciernes*, p. 49). The plunge into the region of unity and enlightenment is suggested by writing but is never totally reached by the scattered signifiers of an unknowable signified. Letting himself go intuitively "en las tinieblas que rodean el conocimiento del hombre" (*En ciernes*, p. 83), the writer must use but also surpass language. The fascinating aspect of Benet's prose, almost perverse in its plodding attachment to implications, allusions, ellusions, and erased/dissimulated inscriptions, is its attempt to comply with the dictum of Bergson that "the art of the writer consists above all in making us forget that he is using the words."[23] Language, therefore, is an expedient means, the finger that points to the moon, the written menu that incites more than placates hunger.

(5) Intellectual freedom may be gained through the interruption of the unmediated reflex act by the instance of memory, which in turn suggests the creation of new responses and the blocking of certain others.[24] Intelligence, here a deep, ultimately unknowable intelligence, saves life from the reiteration of instinct. Most of *Un viaje de invierno* is given over to the capacity, concretized by nature (who brings back Coré, the spring, the same yet different, with no memory to use in comparing), to repeat a party without falling into the numbness of ritual, keeping open to all the unexpected in life (but without falling into the trap of expecting the unexpected).

A searching monologue, an almost imperceptible, sometimes unspoken, dialogue, the embracing in one instant of the duration of a whole life are acts which, like flowing rivers that know no stagnation, long for (and sometimes reach) a shore of rest. Benet's texts have a strong undercurrent of thought that goes beyond mere psychoanalysis and finds its eruption in action. Analytical narration is not idle, therefore, but constitutes verbal action, where all originates and is ultimately resolved.

The essential arguments of Bergson's philosophy are elaborated in dramatic terms that find their way easily into novels: the active presence of the past in the present (of memory in perception), the exhaustion of the soul confronted by the resistance of matter, and the privilege of certain instants of great duration and profoundness that make freedom possible. Benet will incorporate these elements into his work, giving them a characteristic and unique imprint when he pushes to the extreme the frustrations of the soul and the tangles of the mind. While for Faulkner there remains "some bitter and implacable reserve of undefeat" (*Absalom*, p. ll), Benet's characters appear vanquished, resigned, except for the fact that in them memory becomes fantasy and starts a subconscious process that forces them to perceive clearly the victory that could have been theirs. From that image of victory they receive a bitter consolation: "la memoria . . . es casi siempre la venganza de lo que no fue" (*Volverás*, p. 110), or "todo lo que nos queda es lo que un día no pasó"

(p. 288), or even "el tiempo es todo lo que no somos" (p. 279). Faulkner too has written that there is "a might-have-been which is more true than truth" (*Absalom*, p. 143). The soul, never quite resigning itself to the deterioration of the body and the geography in which it finds itself, manifests its force in an imaginative writing that corrects, amplifies, and censors memory, letting it be known that all is not lost, since at least *that* free act is always possible. (In contrast, in *Tiempo de silencio* the mental yoga of Pedro does not alter in any way the fact that he is in jail. The comparison between Martín-Santos's and Benet's attitude toward imagination could be expanded to include their different views of style: the irony of the first stands in sharp contrast to the almost religious cultivation of refinement and difficulty of the second. In Benet one finds a strange, rather old-fashioned belief in the capacity of words to matter, and this confidence has created some of the most brilliant prose of this century. Again, as a contrast, one can consider the deconstructive effort of Juan Goytisolo, who, in his recent fiction, sets out to show the radical contamination of a language that Benet seems to recover unpolluted.)

It is impossible to define further which in Benet are Faulknerian influences and which ideas are derived from his direct reading of Bergson. One should not forget, however, Benet's own originality nor neglect the opportunities for simple coincidences provided by a common system of questions. But it is evident that Benet found in Faulkner, and especially in their common mentor, Bergson, the formulation for certain philosophical questions that would become central to his narrative.

There are at least two other conclusions that can be drawn from this study, and both are of immediate usefulness. The first conclusion refers to how Benet can be read in Latin America. Readers there will understand his work better if they associate it with the novels of García Márquez, Roa Bastos, Vargas Llosa, or Carpentier, and, especially, with the writing of Borges, instead of with other Spanish writers like Cela, Delibes, or Juan Goytisolo. The second conclusion pertains to those critics who frown at the extreme slowness and deliberation of Benet's texts, the flatness of his characters, and the confusing, enigmatic, and truncated story lines, three characteristics that can be reinterpreted when the origin and originality of Benet's narrative world is understood. Recently Benet declared to *El País Semanal* that to write a novel with a story line is the easiest thing in the world. Once sketched, the argument itself and the characters drag the writer behind them, like horses from their bridles. What is really difficult is to write a novel without a story line.[25] Our insight into his links to Faulkner and Bergson has determined that, indeed, in Benet's work the story line is not to be found in the anecdote, but at another level in which the protagonists are perception, time, duration, and, above all, an active, imaginative, deceptive, and liberating memory.

ROBERTO C. MANTEIGA

# Time, Space, and Narration in
# Juan Benet's Short Stories

Juan Benet's short stories are generally as complex and enigmatic as
his novels.[1] Indeed, some of the stories—and the author prides himself on this fact—are virtually incomprehensible. What makes
Benet's short fiction so difficult, in addition to the rambling style
and complicated syntax that characterize nearly all of his writings,
are the temporal and spatial complexities of the narrative. My essay
will address the questions of time and space in Benet's short fiction
in an attempt to determine whether the author follows the Bergsonian model, as other critics have suggested, or whether he offers
new insights into time and space that go beyond Bergson.[2] I have
chosen not to include in my analysis all of Benet's stories but rather
shall focus on those works in which time and space are acutely relevant to theme or structure.[3]

First, it is necessary to distinguish between Benet's treatment of
linear time and novelistic or subjective time. Let us first examine the
former. Much of Benet's shorter fiction (and, indeed, nearly all of
his literary works) can be described in structural terms as a series of
events out of time.[4] The narrative technique he employs is not unlike the technique employed by Alain Robbe-Grillet. Yet whereas
Robbe-Grillet attempts to isolate or frame moments in time much
in the same manner as the lens of a camera, Benet creates more of a
cinematic effect. Benet is like a projectionist who, prior to showing
a movie, removes the film from the spool, stretches it out, and indis-
criminately cuts it into sections. After discarding what he does not

want, he rearranges the sections, splices the film back together, rolls it back onto the spool and proceeds to show the movie. Not only is the concept of linear time destroyed, but huge gaps are left in the story line.

The question of subjective time is far more complex. As a number of Benet scholars have already pointed out, at the heart of Benet's philosophy of time is the Bergsonian idea of *durée*, best defined perhaps by the saxophonist in Julio Cortázar's *El perseguidor* as that essential instant in time that allows us to live a thousand times longer than we are presently living with the clock. Bergson defined time as a medium in which feelings, impressions, and emotions are arranged in the same kind of order that we find in space— that is, one after the other. Time marks our conscious existence in space and is thus measurable or homogeneous. *Durée*, on the other hand, is concerned with the sensations experienced by a body in space. It differs from homogeneous time in that it is immeasurable and has nothing to do with space itself.[5] Based on this supposition, Bergson concluded that there are two kinds of memory: memory of habit (our conscious recollection) and true memory, which records every moment of duration and takes place on a continuing basis.[6] The influence of Bergson can be seen in particular in the works of three novelists who have had a substantial effect on Benet's own development as a writer: Marcel Proust, William Faulkner, and the previously mentioned Robbe-Grillet.

Based in large part on the studies of Bergson, Marcel Proust developed his theory of *mémoire involontaire*. While Proust disagreed somewhat with Bergson's conclusion that time and space are inseparable—real time, according to Proust, lives within us and is not imposed upon us by space—he did, nevertheless, accept Bergson's ideas with respect to the two kinds of memory, one marked by time and the other by *durée*. In addition Proust believed that the true past is hidden somewhere beyond the reach of the intellect and can only be recalled through sensory perceptions.[7] As will be shown, Benet frequently alludes to the Proustian idea of *mémoire involontaire* in his stories. His characters often discover hidden secrets about themselves through involuntary lapses.

In William Faulkner's works there is a very real sense of Bergson's

*durée*. Faulkner saw time as "a fluid condition which has no existence except in the momentary avatars of individual people."[8] He
argued that "there is no time, there is only the present moment in
which I include both the past and the future, and that is eternity."[9]
In Faulkner the present is marked by the "super presence" of a
highly charged past that Patricia Drechsel Tobin calls the "absolute
past."[10] This absolute past is both obsessive and oppressive, as well
as regressive, in that it recalls events that are indefinable within the
context of chronological time. For Benet, as for Faulkner, time is
fluid: an ever-elusive present haunted by an oppressive past plunges
headlong into an uncertain future. Isolated moments from the past
continually return to haunt Benet's characters. This idea of doomed
repetition recurs throughout the stories I will examine. In some
cases Benet's characters become trapped in that moment of *durée*,
and thus chronological time ceases to exist for them. This concept,
which I refer to as "frozen time," and which Benet calls "el espíritu
de la porcelana,"[11] is, I believe, the most original facet of Benet's
treatment of time and space.

For Alain Robbe-Grillet time exists exclusively as an aspect of
space. He creates in his works a camera effect that he calls *temps-
manqué*. The camera first destroys linear time, collapses it into isolated and crucial moments, then "draws" an abstract shape that
bears a specific relationship to the theme of the work. "A novel created in this way," says Sharon Spencer, "is not a record made with
words but an impression that remains in the reader's mind as the
illusion of a form."[12] Benet is equally successful in isolating or
painting images of key moments, reproducing with cinematographic exactness such temporal effects as time shift and fade in/
fade out. In addition, he often superimposes one image on another,
thus creating a photomontage effect.

It is imperative when studying the question of time and space in a
literary work to consider as well the narrative devices used by the
author. In Benet's short stories there are three basic types of narrative voices, all of which have one element in common: they are all,
to a certain degree, unreliable. The most common is the third-
person editorial narrator who, unlike most narrators of this kind,
often reports from hearsay, withholds information from the reader,

has lapses of memory, and doubts about names of people, places, dates, and other important facts. This narrator is also given to philosophizing, making generalizations, and commenting on the discourse of the characters. These same traits characterize Benet's first-person narrators. They too withhold information, report from hearsay, and are prone to forget important facts, leaving the reader with some of the same doubts that they appear to have.

Another narrative voice Benet employs with a great deal of skill is what Seymour Chatman calls the "covert narrator": "a voice speaking of events, characters and setting but hidden in the discursive shadows." [13] This type of third-person narrator expresses the character's speech or thought in indirect form, that is, he verbalizes the character's perceptions. [14] Benet's covert narrator, however, is equally unreliable, expressing indirectly the characters' doubts, apprehensions, twisted ideas, and malicious intentions, a possibility not considered in Chatman's own definition of unreliable narration. [15]

The presence of unreliable and contradicting narrators, coupled with the fact that in so many of Benet's short stories much of the story line is missing, forces the reader to draw narrative inferences of his own. This type of narrative filling-in, or what the structuralists refer to as reading out, is a necessary exercise in understanding Benet's fiction. The author does, however, provide the reader with a number of aids that make this reading-out process somewhat easier. The most common is the use of leitmotivs, directly associated with a particular character or situation and repeated sufficiently throughout the story to give the reader a point of orientation. Other more concrete means of orienting the reader include giving dates, place names, and making references to certain characters that interact throughout the story.

The first group of stories I will examine are those that take place in that intricate spatial and temporal labyrinth known as Región. [16] David K. Herzberger has accurately described Región as an enigmatic region "in a full state of decadence, surrounded by hostile landscapes and immersed in a threatening temperate zone." [17] Clocks serve no purpose in Región, for time is not measured by machines but by the "mechanism of the human psyche." [18] Because the ruinous and decadent past weighs so heavily on the consciousness of the inhabitants of Región, their lives are marked by a sense of doomed repetition. This idea of doomed repetition appears in nearly all of the Región stories and forms the central motif of Benet's fiction.

"Una tumba," an intriguing account of a class struggle pitting the vengeance of the working class against the tyranny of a wealthy landowner, is, in fact, a short novel and is treated as such by David K. Herzberger. The story concerns the fate of a young boy presently living with the caretaker of the boy's family estate. The boy's great-grandfather, referred to only as the Brigadier, was assassinated in a Rasputin-like manner by a group of political adversaries in the year 1884 (one of the few references to chronological time in the story).[19] Sometime after his death the Brigadier's tomb was ransacked and his body stolen. The grave, which remained open, serves as a leitmotiv or a reminder of the fate that awaits the young boy.[20]

In "Reichenau" (the title is a reference to a town in Germany) the idea of doomed repetition surfaces once again. A third person omniscient narrator tells the story of a man who one evening becomes lost on the labyrinthine roads leading to Región and decides to spend the night at a hostel. He experiences a sleepless night, haunted by a nightmarish series of events. At times he feels tempted to call the owner, but something restrains him. Upon paying the bill the next morning, the owner points out to him that by ringing the bell he could have saved himself a sleepless night. Sometime later while traveling in Germany he checks into a hotel in the town of Reichenau, near Lake Constance, and relives the same experience. This time, however, he manages to reach the bell, but just as he rings it he hears footsteps, the doorknob begins to turn, and he flashes back upon the image of a papier-mâché head that appears to him from a remote past. The reader is not told whether the image corresponds to a childhood experience or to a mythical situation that could have taken place in another place and at another time. The text suggests, nonetheless, that the man's sudden realization that he has experienced this before coincides with his death.

The concept of doomed repetition, as well as the introduction of other temporal themes, clearly shapes the narrative of "Después." Although not included in volume one of Cuentos completos with the other Región stories, it is evident that it too takes place in that enigmatic and mythical space. The story's temporal complexities, clearly Proustian in nature, coupled with the author's unique narrative devices, make "Después" one of Benet's most challenging pieces of short fiction.

The story is narrated in the third person by what appears to be an omniscient narrator. Upon closer scrutiny, however, we find that, while the narrator is capable of penetrating the psyche of his characters and revealing their innermost thoughts, he nevertheless has doubts with respect to these very same characters. He is thus given to conjecture: "Debían beber bastante" (2:143); "Pocas personas—acaso sólo una—debían comprender hasta donde llegaba esa mirada" (2:143); "Tal vez creyeran que tras aquel silencio . . . había algo" (2:145). In addition, the narrator quite often philosophizes, makes judgments or comments on his own discourse or on the discourse of his characters: "Tan sólo se trataba, decía el viejo, de saber esperar ('si han de venir, ya vendrán'), si se está esperando y se sabe esperar más de lo que se debe puede incluso que no pase nada y se encuentre . . . la eternidad" (2:145).[21]

The actual duration of the story could very well be a matter of minutes or even seconds. It begins with "llamaron de nuevo" (2:141) and ends with "Abrió, al fin, la puerta del jardín, escondiendo la cara. 'Pasen, por favor, pasen'" (2:164). The novelistic time, however, is at least a quarter of a century, and there are allusions to things that occurred long before that.

"Después" is the story of a house in a ruinous state, and of the two men who inhabit it, one older than the other. The men never leave the house, never answer the door, and the garden gate is bolted closed year round: "se hubieran dejado de recibir visitas o recados desde tiempo inmemorial" (2:141). The only known callers to the house in recent years have been the woman who brought them their food, the man who delivered the wine, Dr. Sebastián, and the mysterious "mujer de la venganza," "que muchas tardes se acercaba al lugar, envuelta en un abrigo y con un pañuelo anudado a la cabeza, para mirar desde detrás de los árboles" (2:144). Inside the house hangs a clock that never keeps the right time, but whose silence makes the men uneasy. Whenever it stops ticking one of the

men stands on a chair and winds it. Should by coincidence the
chime ring the two men lean back in their chairs and slip into a moment of brief ecstasy of love and sorrow over their lost childhood.
They do nothing all day but sit and drink, lost somewhere between
a mysterious past and a foreboding future. The narrative strongly
suggests that someone or something is going to take revenge on the
house. In the meantime, the two men just wait.

The younger of the two men (in his forties) is either retarded or
insane and given to violent behavior. The narrator speaks of the
man's *vicio* and *enfermedad*. We know too that in his youth this
man committed a heinous crime. While the narrator never specifies
the nature of this crime, there are strong suggestions that he raped
and killed someone. The narrator speaks of "la familia de la víc-
tima," and the image of "una espalda desnuda" is continually conjured up. The boy's father, in order to avoid a repetition of the scandal, entrusts his son to the care of a friend, a man somewhat older
than his son. Because the father's house holds so many bad memories for the boy, he and the older man are moved into another house
where they remain locked up like prisoners.

When the father dies the old man becomes the son's legal guardian. The father's friends and business acquaintances believe that the
son should preside at his father's funeral. But since it is the first time
he is to leave the house they take every precaution to avoid a new
manifestation of the "illness." Following the ceremony, they go to
the father's house for the reading of the will, where vivid memories
come back to haunt the son. The ensuing scenes are so bizarre that
the reader is unable to determine whether they are real or purely
allegorical.

In one scene an unidentified woman disrobes, lets down her hair,
and tempts the son into bed. The guardian physically struggles with
the son to try to keep him away from the woman, shouting to him,
"No es la misma. No es la misma. No es la misma. ¿No ves que no
es la misma? Te digo que no es la misma" (2:156). When the fighting ends the old man looks over at the woman in the bed and tells
the son,

"Ahí la tienes. Ya lo has conseguido. Ahí la tienes; luego volveremos a
casa. Pero si fueras hombre de verdad no lo harías, justamente porque ser

hombre significa haber adquirido la fuerza suficiente para no dar un paso hacia allá . . . porque eso que tienes ahí delante . . . mezclado con perfumes de almohada y cabelleras sueltas . . . no es más que la encerrona que una muerte apercibida de tu próximo despertar te tiene preparada día tras día. Porque eso es la muerte: vivir ese instante dominado tan sólo por ese instante. Este es seguramente tu primer encuentro con ella, pero volverá más veces; te acuerdas todavía de los campanillazos en las tardes húmedas con la interrogante sobre las aguas de fuera; es la muerte, en un instante resucitada. Un día sabrás lo que es eso, sabrás lo que es vivir, algo que sólo se sabe cuando ella ronda el ambiente, porque todo lo demás es inútil, es costumbre y es pasado; el presente, esa parte del tiempo arbitraria, irresponsable, cruel, involuntaria y extraña a ti, tan falsa que de un solo guiño te convertirá en un cadáver, tan estimable que el día que la puedas sobrevivir te harás un hombre y sabrás vivir. . . . Si sales triunfante te aseguro que ninguna llamada volverá a turbar la paz de nuestra siesta. (2 : 159–60)

The woman in this scene is both a symbol of the son's own voluntary entrapment as well as the personification of death. By not giving in to her, he can free himself from the prison he had created for himself. Yet, despite all of the old man's efforts to deter him, the son succumbs.

The following morning the two men return home. They continue to have callers but refuse to answer. One afternoon, however, someone knocks in a very peculiar manner. The old man opens the rear door to the house and beckons the visitor to come in. Water fills the house, a coffin is seen floating in the hallway, and a young boy runs through the hallway chasing a little white ball. The many symbols lead us to believe that the son has died. Death was the liberation he had been patiently awaiting all along. Ironically its arrival coincides with the flood, a symbol of life. Happiness (the boy playing with the ball) returns after years of gloom.

In "Duelo" the idea of "doomed repetition" once again functions as a thematic and structural device. The story itself develops around the ritualistic visit of two men identified only as Don Lucas and Blanco every July twelfth to the gravesite of a woman named Rosa. This scene, which constitutes all of section I and which is repeated again at the end of section VIII, appears to be the now of the story and corresponds chronologically to about 1960. The other sections, II through VII, are flashbacks marked by numerous time shifts. Since so much of the story line is omitted (one of Benet's techniques mentioned earlier), it is difficult to reconstruct. The reader is, nonetheless, able to piece together the scant story line and identify the characters in certain scenes through numerous leitmotivs.[22]

The uniqueness of "Duelo" lies in Benet's development of two possible plots (in the manner of Borges), each replete with its own series of bound motifs. On the one hand the reader is led to believe that the protagonist, Don Lucas, courts Rosa and restores the house at Nueva Elvira out of a fatherly concern for the girl. We come to learn, however, that this is not the case, but that he is in fact motivated by vengeance. Yet only through repeated references to Don Lucas's obsession with the idea of purity and innocence, and by the narrator's allusion to a certain betrayal by a former lover, which looms as one of those "instantes gigantescos"[23] in Benet's fiction, do we become convinced of his more sinister intentions. The numerous time shifts, the gaps in the story line, the question of psychological time as it concerns the principal characters, and, of course, the idea of "doomed repetition" as conveyed by the yearly ritual of visiting the gravesite, make "Duelo" one of Benet's most complex and imaginative short stories.

The technique of developing two possible story lines can be seen also in "Una línea incompleta." The story concerns a certain César Abrantes, a student of minerology living in London. On a visit home to Región, César falls in love with a girl whom he plans to marry against his father's strong objections. After some irregular correspondence between them, César learns of his fiancée's untimely death. When he still continues to receive letters from her he becomes suspicious and decides to report the matter to the police, who then investigate the situation. Part of the story is narrated in English by one of the investigators who recounts the events as told to him by César Abrantes. Another part of the story is related by a third-person narrator who reconstructs for us the history of the two families, the Abrantes and the Queiles families (Queiles is the girl's family). The narrator's doubts concerning the lives of these people is revealed by a discourse replete with such uncertainties as, "It is possible that," "no one remembers precisely," and "it has been in-sinuated that."

From this rather broken narration we are able to deduce that César Abrantes's father, Honorio, and the girl's stepfather, Mr. Queiles, were at one time involved in a land war, that the paternity of both César and the girl is uncertain,[24] and that a third party had been intercepting and changing the contents of the letters to and from England. One of the letters, which was later discovered by the investigators and eventually attached to their report, was a letter mailed in London. Attributed to César but written by someone else, the last line of the letter was left incomplete, ending abruptly far from the right-hand margin. We assume, therefore, that whoever was intercepting the letters and substituting his own, was murdered before he had a chance to finish writing this last one.

As previously mentioned, the story is constructed on the basis of two possible story lines. At first, the reader is led to believe that César and the girl are half-brothers and that Honorio acts honorably in trying to put an end to a potentially incestuous relationship. Later we learn that there is strong evidence to prove that the two are not related and that the true reason for the girl's death is the greed of her stepfather and Honorio Abrantes. If this were not enough, we discover that it is not the girl's death that we should be primarily concerned with, but that of the mysterious third party who had been intercepting and altering the contents of the letters.

Although the idea of doomed repetition represents the essential temporal concern of Benet in the Región stories, the question of time is treated in other ways as well. In "De lejos," for example, the author fuses his temporal concerns with the narration itself. The story begins with the narrator describing a family dinner that took place some time in the past. From the assumptions made by the narrator we presume that he was present at the dinner but did not know the people very well at the time: "No era un hombre de mucha edad, pero parecía retirado; más tarde vine a saber que no era así, sino que, con una salud bastante quebrantada, se limitaba en aquella época a seguir de cerca las pocas inversiones en que había cristalizado su carrera en activo" (1 : 145). Neither the narrator nor any of the family members are named. They are simply referred to as *padre, hijo mayor*, and so forth. The principal narrator recalls conversations in detail almost as if he had had a tape recorder with him at the dinner table, which he is now playing back for the "narratee." [25] The narration switches from a third- to a first-person narrator (the father) who relates an episode in his life. Although the words are the father's we never lose sight of the fact that all this is being told to us secondhand by the principal narrator. Mixed in with this portion of the narrative are periodic interjections such as "más hielo, por favor," "No, no es tarde," "¿Se han acostado?", and "No me interrumpas," which return the disconcerted reader to the now of the father's narration. An even more ingenious narrative technique is the parallel the author creates between the duration of the father's monologue and the nature of his interjections, many of which refer to the fact that the contents of the bottle from which he is drinking are gradually being consumed —"Un poco más, lo que queda," "Apenas queda nada," and finally "Parece que ya no queda nada"—words that coincide with the final words of one of the characters in the father's tale.

The father's story is autobiographical in nature and tells of an experience he had in his youth. Soon after his graduation from school he went to work for a highly respected colleague, Conrado Blaer, "mucho mayor que nosotros, claro está, en algunos círculos profesionales tenía fama de hombre excéntrico y vagabundo, con algo de mago y bastante de loco" (1:148). Although involved in a mining operation that Blaer was directing the father never really meets the man. His recollections of Blaer are veiled in mystery, and his comments regarding the man's very existence are suspect. On one occasion he states, "Pues bien, era Blaer; me lo he dicho y repetido mil veces, todavía no he cansado de afirmarlo. . . Era Blaer, lo repetiré mientras viva; lo único que no tenía de Blaer era . . . su presencia física" (1:158–59). After a supposed second visit when he recalls seeing Blaer wrapped in a blanket and tending a fire he comments, "A la mañana siguiente había desaparecido sin dejar el menor indicio de su vivac; ni las mantas ni las señales del fuego" (1:161).

In reality Blaer is nothing more than an enigma. He is not a man of flesh and blood but a concept: the father's alter ego, the incarnation of a work ideal that lives within him. The altruistic father, who had joined the mining operation in hopes of making a lot of money, ends up disillusioned and broke with Blaer's final words to him ringing in his ears: "No queda nada" (1 : 166).

In the short stories examined thus far, we have seen that the Bergsonian concept of time is central to Benet's own treatment of time and space. While it cannot be said that the idea of chronological time is of no concern to the author, he does, nevertheless, place a great deal more emphasis on subjective or psychological time, on the ability of the consciousness of his characters to recapture past moments. The characters' pasts weigh heavily on their lives and come back to haunt them time and again. The most common manifestations of this are, as we have seen, the ideas of doomed repetition and foreboding prophesy. In the short stories that comprise volume two of the *Cuentos completos* many of these same ideas are repeated. In addition, however, Benet poses certain philosophical questions with respect to time and space that go beyond Bergson. Furthermore, Benet draws upon cinematographic-like techniques in order to duplicate in print the numerous time shifts, photomontages, and fade-ins/fade-outs that we are accustomed to seeing on the screen.

In his book *Tiempo y narración*, Pedro Ramírez Molas discusses a concept that he calls *instante vital*, and which he defines as that moment when a person turns within himself and concentrates all of his energies on a unique and vital goal.[26] "El instante," says Ramírez Molas, "es extático en sí mismo porque rompe la continuidad de la sucesión y coagula el pretérito, el presente y el futuro en un tiempo en el que no cuentan el antes ni el después."[27] He cites as examples a number of characters from the short stories of Jorge Luis Borges, including Emma Zunz, for whom the idea of vengeance becomes the single force justifying her existence. This *instante vital* is a moment so profound that life and death actually merge as one. Likewise, in Borges's "El hacedor," when the protagonist returns to the home in which he was born, the narrator remarks, "yo querría saber que sintió en aquel instante de vértigo en que el pasado y el presente se confundieron; yo querría saber si el hijo perdido renació y murió en aquel éxtasis."[28]

The idea of *instante vital* or frozen time, is clearly manifested in

the short story "Ultimas noches de un invierno húmedo." Related in
the third person by an omniscient narrator, the story centers on
Señor Martín, a recent widower suffering from a terrible case of
bronchitis and loneliness. His daughter decides that for health reasons her father should spend the damp winter months in a warmer
climate, and rents a room for him in a hotel on the coast. There he
lives a relatively isolated existence and has little or no contact with
his neighbors. One afternoon just before lunch, while sitting on his
porch, Señor Martín sees one of the young girls who lives in the
bungalow next door come running out wrapped only in a towel.
Without saying a word she opens the sliding glass door to Señor
Martín's room and sneaks inside. Soon afterward a young man
comes out of the same bungalow looking for the girl. Not finding
her, he gets in his car and drives away. The girl comes out of Señor
Martín's bathroom where she had been hiding and in a gesture of
thanks embraces him, runs her hand through his hair, kisses him,
and then runs off.

For Señor Martín the moment of the girl's embrace is a vital instant, that brings back, in the form of images, memories of his first
sexual experience: "piezas de lencería de color tabaco y negro, el
perfume hediondo" (2:203). From this moment on, all other past
memories begin to fade away. His daughter's voice on the telephone
appears distant and he imagines her in miniature. The only thing
that begins to grow is the sound of the waves as he walks from his
hotel room toward the beach and into the sea. The sexual images
alluded to above become superimposed on the images of the sea
creating a photomontage effect. Thus for Señor Martín time freezes
in that vital instant that marks both his reawakening to life as well
as the moment of his death.

The question of time and space is also uniquely treated in "Catálisis." [29] An older couple living in a resort town anxiously await the
end of the vacation season and the departure of the many tourists
that populate the area. In the off season the town is very peaceful
and the two enjoy strolling during the late afternoon hours. On one
particular afternoon they decide to go as far as the grade crossing, a
bit further than they have ventured in the past. On the way they
pass a man walking his dog. Despite a threatening sky, they decide

to continue, comforted by the fact that there is an inn just around the next bend. Suddenly lightning is perceived and the woman freezes in her tracks. As the old man takes his wife's hand in his he feels her fear pass through him. After the experience, they notice that the man they have just passed appears "inverosimilmente lejos," and they sense that they have gone beyond the inn. Everything around them is unrecognizable: "de igual manera que la fotografía de un paisaje familiar, cuando ha sido revelada al revés, no resulta fácil de identificar porque no esconde ningún engaño" (2:225). The old man suggests they return, but the wife responds, "es inútil." They continue onward yet cover no ground. As the man with the dog passes them by, the last vestiges of their perception allow them to notice for the first time that the man is also carrying a cane and is wearing dark glasses. Like Señor Martín in "Ultimas noches de un invierno húmedo," the couple in this story is trapped in time. They have defied the laws of physics, passing from one space to another in one vital instant, but are now incapable of returning or proceeding. They are prisoners, frozen in that moment out of time, while time, symbolized by the blindman, passes them by.

Some of the stories in the second volume, while not offering any new insights into the question of time, do, nevertheless, treat time in the more traditional Bergsonian sense while concurrently exploring new modes of narration. For example, "Nunca llegarás a nada," published for the first time in 1961, is Benet's earliest fictional work, preceding the Región era by nearly six years. As with the early works of many writers, the influence of other novelists, in Benet's case Proust and Faulkner, is quite apparent. Narrated primarily in the past tense by a first-person narrator identified only as Juan, the story concerns a trip he and his friend Vicente took to Paris, the subsequent illicit involvement of Vicente with a French woman, the trio's escape from Paris and interminable rides on the trains of Europe, and the murder of a mysterious man at the hands of Vicente, culminating in the latter's arrest.

The title is taken from the words of the narrator's aunt Juana expressed to the young man some years earlier: "Calamidad, nunca llegarás a nada" (p. 60). We assume that the narrator's parents died and that he was raised by his aunt, a rather stern woman for whom he has somewhat less than fond memories. The narrator often expresses regret over the fact that he never had a family, which he views in a rather Proustian sense as a comfort and consolation to an individual:

> Para aquellas personas que no tienen familia . . . debe amanecer un día. . . en que el pasado familiar manda. . . sin duda amanece un día en que. . . emerge el pasado en un momento de incertidumbre para exorcizar el tiempo maligno y sórdido y volver a traer la serenidad, ridiculizando y desbaratando la frágil y estéril, quimérica e insatisfecha condición de un presente torturado y andarín, eternamente absorto en el vuelo de una mosca en torno a una tulipa verde. (2:64)

The words of the narrator's aunt eventually loom prophetic. He has a great deal of difficulty holding down a decent job and eventually finds himself working for someone involved in shady dealings. He decides to leave this job and go to Paris with his rich friend Vicente, who agrees to pay his way. The narrator's recollections of the trip and of the time that preceded it are extremely vague. All sense of chronological time is lost. Scenes from the narrator's past fade in and fade out like the scenes on a movie screen. One moment he remembers being at his friend Vera's house in Madrid, and the next moment he is in Paris. This cinematographic effect is skillfully duplicated in Benet's narrative: "Habíamos hecho todos los esfuerzos imaginables para encender la chimenea de Vera; apenas logramos otra cosa que prender unas astillas y atufar la habitación con un humo agrio cuando, con el vuelo de unas cenizas de papel, cortando la narración, el tiempo falso se hincha y nos lleva al apartamento de París" (2:69). In typical Faulknerian style the narrator explains: "Lo cierto es que si aquella misma madrugada, al salir de su casa y tomar un taxi desvencijado, no salimos para París fue porque, desgraciadamente, hay un tiempo fluido que enlaza y separa todos los sucesos. Lo que pasa en ese tiempo nadie lo sabe: ni se recuerda ni se prevé" (2:69).

This fade-in and fade-out technique often occurs with great rapidity, as in the following segment in which the narrator talks about the image of a woman's hair that has become an obsession with him:

No sé cuánto tiempo me pasé aproximándome a aquel pelo, no tanto en aquel sofá como en la cama del hotel, repasando sin memoria las latas de pintura y dejando consumir las horas en una bomba vieja de bicicleta; en los departamentos de tercera, haciendo confidencias a un viajero sentimental, que, al menos, sabía consolarme en el más puro estilo parlamentario, y mirando los papeles pintados y los pájaros japoneses decapitados por los boquetes donde asomaba el revoco, y muy cerca del despertar, años después, cuando su cara, a los golpes de la virtud y la avaricia, se iba afilando para cruzar el pasillo en sombras—se diría—sin necesidad de andar sobre las zapatillas, ¿cómo iba a explicarle al espectro de mi tía que en gran parte se debía al olor propio de un pelo sin brillo que había vislumbrado meses atrás? (2:74–75).

The Proustian idea of involuntary memory is present throughout the story. One day when the narrator sees the frozen liver paté that his hostess at the hotel in Paris is cutting, he comments, "Cuando empezó a cortar el extracto de hígado gelatinoso y horrendo de mi memoria infantil, hizo saltar en mi interior toda la insuficiente banalidad de una tarde acidulada de pasión. . . toda la obsesión de un aburrimiento infantil, temporalmente olvidado al friso de los quince años para reaparecer a la vuelta de los treinta" (2:85). The most frequently recurring example of involuntary memory is the image previously alluded to of the dark and lifeless hair of the woman. This image (perhaps the only thing the narrator remembers about his mother) is conjured up in his mind every time he sees a woman with similar hair.

Numerous time shifts, the presence of several narrators, and echoes of Proust and Faulkner manifest themselves throughout the author's work. As we have seen, Benet is far more interested in the psychological time of his characters (the Bergsonian idea of *durée*) than he is in the idea of chronological time. Like Faulkner, Benet believes that time is fluid. The present is ever changing, ever elusive, ever approaching an uncertain future. The past weighs heavily on the present and becomes an obsession with many of Benet's characters. Isolated moments from the characters' pasts come back to haunt them time and again. This idea of doomed repetition is central to the author's philosophy of time and is repeated throughout his work. For some of Benet's characters the past is all that exists.

They become frozen in time, forced to relive continually a particular moment from their past. This vital instant, as Ramírez Molas calls it, is a moment of ecstasy in which life and death actually become one. Thus, while Benet's philosophy of time and space follows more or less Bergsonian lines, he touches upon questions that are more metaphysical than many of Bergson's own perceptions of time.

In terms of style and technique Benet is as innovative and daring as Robbe-Grillet. Like the French novelist and critic, Benet is a master at capturing and isolating moments in time and at forming images or impressions of these moments that remain etched in the reader's mind. He is successful as well in duplicating through his use of words even more complex cinematographic techniques such as fade-in/fade-out and photomontage. In addition Benet employs a number of equally subjective narrative voices, some of which contradict one another. Even those narrators who appear to be omniscient often prove unreliable. The result is a group of short stories so enigmatic that even the most discerning reader finds them difficult to comprehend. This is not surprising, however, since the author's objective is very often to create a work that expresses his view of reality. For Benet, there is no true picture of reality, only individual perceptions that are limited in scope and colored by one's emotions. As an author, Benet is more concerned with that enigmatic side of reality; those aspects we know least about (what the author himself calls the shadowy zone). Since no one individual is capable of knowing everything, why should the reader, therefore, assume that an author's work is going to supply him with all of the answers? Benet's work certainly does not, but it indeed provokes a number of complex questions.

# Notes

*Robert C. Spires: Juan Benet's Poetics of Open Spaces*

1. Juan Benet, *En ciernes* (Madrid: Taurus, 1976) and *El ángel del Señor abandona a Tobías* (Barcelona: La Gaya Ciencia, 1976). All quotes from these editions will be given in parentheses in the text.

*Malcolm Alan Compitello: The Paradoxes of Praxis: Juan Benet and Modern Poetics*

1. A listing of Benet's essays can be found in the Bibliography. David K. Herzberger has produced the most substantial and important body of scholarship dealing with Benet as theorist. My study "Ordering the Evidence: The Vision of the Spanish Civil War in Post-War Spanish Fiction" (in press, Ediciones Puvill) treats Benet as literary critic and cultural critic of contemporary Spain.

2. See, for example, Benet's "Contra James Joyce," *Informaciones de las Artes y las Letras*, 9 July 1970, pp. 1–2, and his interview with Eduardo García Rico, "Juan Benet: Joyce es de segunda fila," *Triunfo*, no. 249 (22 August 1970), p. 2.

3. Answers to *encuesta* on literature and education in Spain, *Literatura y educación*, ed. Fernando Lázaro Carreter (Madrid: Castalia, 1974), p. 204. Similar views are found in his essay "El crítico hombre del orden," *Índice*, nos. 301–302 (January-February 1972), p. 41. For Benet's view of Chomskian linguistics see *El angel del Señor abandona a Tobías* (Barcelona: La Gaya Ciencia, 1976). The work should be read in conjunction with David K. Herzberger's perceptive analysis of its shortcomings in his book review published in *American Hispanist*, 2, no. 16 (March 1977), pp. 16–17.

4. At times it appears that Benet tends to confuse the roles of literary criticism and theory, which, I maintain, are activities that exist at two different levels of operation.

5. I refer to his participation in the "Mesa redonda sobre la novela" organized by *Cuadernos para el Diálogo* and published by that journal in a special issue, 23 (December 1970), pp. 45–52. Benet's interventions so incensed moderator Isaac Montero that he wrote a reply to Benet, "Acotaciones a una mesa redonda: respuestas a Juan Benet y defensa apresurada del realismo," published in the same issue of *Cuadernos* (pp. 65–74), along with Benet's answer to Montero's objections, "Respuesta al señor Montero" (pp. 75–76). The issue also contains Benet's "Reflexiones sobre Galdós," a highly critical assessment of the Spanish novelist (pp. 13–15).

6. All quotes from *La inspiración y el estilo* are taken from the Seix Barral edition (Barcelona, 1973). Citations will be given in parentheses in the text. At this juncture I should add that David K. Herzberger sees another formative component in Benet's view of literature: enigma. He has studied its function in a number of essays. The most important are "Enigma as Narrative Determinant in Juan Benet," *Hispanic Review*, 47 (1979), pp. 149–157, for Benet's narrative; and "Theoretical Approaches to the Spanish New Novel: Juan Benet and Juan Goytisolo," *Revista de Estudios Hispánicos*, 14, no. 2 (1980), pp. 3–17, for theory.

7. In an interview by Federico Campbell, "Juan Benet o el azar," in *Infame turba* (Barcelona: Lumen, 1971), pp. 293–310, the novelist responded in the following manner to Campbell's question about the importance of inspiration in his work:

Sí, por eso hice un libro sobre el tema. Pero la inspiración viene sólo a condición de que haya estilo. Inspiración y estilo vienen a ser prácticamente compenetrables e identificables. La inspiración dicta. Ese dictado se siente como algo ineluctable, algo revelado. Tal como viene hay que ponerlo en el papel. Para que esa inspiración sea verdaderamente válida, hay que reconocer que dicta en un estilo determinado que además predetermina el estilo venidero; eso es muy evidente en las composiciones líricas, que por lo general siempre tienen un verso inspirado. Pero la inspiración dicta poco, y hay que darle la redondez y componer. Esa labor de composición es ya el trabajo propio de un escritor, que tiene que alcanzar la cosa por sí mismo, con su propio trabajo y esfuerzo, la cosa que le ha sido dado casi sin trabajo. La inspiración dicta ya con estilo, y para mí es evidente, la inspiración dicta de una manera que ya no se puede alterar. Lo que no sea eso no es inspiración. Dicta un verso y ese verso tiene que ser tal como lo vio el poeta, o tal como lo oyó. Le dicta la primera frase de una narración, y hay que ponerla tal como fue escuchada, luego hay que seguir, y al final, la síntesis de esa dialéctica entre inspiración y ejecución del estilo viene a resumirse cuando la inspiración es de tal índole que dicta en un estilo muy regular, que es lo mismo que ayudó a forjar. (pp. 309–310)

8. The following passage from *La inspiración y el estilo* demonstrates the difference between the two sets of relationships:

Si se cotejan dos a dos esas categorías se debe concluir que en comparación con el contenido la información es un concepto más específico y reducido. No se puede llamar información todo lo que dice el escritor, sino a aquello que dice con cierto propósito de docencia, aprovechando el desnivel entre sus conocimientos y la ignorancia del lector. La forma se relaciona solamente con la estructura de la frase, con la selección de las palabras y la modulación del significado; pero el estilo es mucho más vasto porque toma sobre sí no sólo todas las modalidades de dicción, sino el interés de toda la información. Dentro de ese complicado organismo el estilo asume todas las funciones dinámicas y se configura como un sistema que aprovecha el desnivel originado por la información para crear un movimiento de interés, que mantiene su marcha incluso por inercia, cuando aquel desnivel se anula. (p. 139)

9. Campbell, "Juan Benet o el azar," p. 325.

10. For a full discussion of this point see the essays "La entrada en la taberna" and "La ofensiva de 1850" in *La inspiración y el estilo*.

11. "Porque la literatura, como la pintura, como la arquitectura, maneja una segunda realidad, y esta segunda realidad es tan firme y tan inconclusa

como la primera realidad. La literatura maneja un sistema de representaciones; no maneja ni este cenicero, sino una segunda realidad. Esa segunda realidad puede no tener las mismas leyes de la primera realidad en que vivimos pero tiene otras" (Campbell, "Juan Benet o el azar," p. 303).

12. Ibid., p. 302.

13. As he remarks during the "Mesa redonda sobre la novela": "Para él la literatura es una especie de refugio maldito donde se ha tenido que recluir por circunstancias personales, por circunstancias históricas o porque no ha podido tener una beca para dedicarse a la electrónica" (p. 52).

14. From Roman Jacobson, "Recent Russian Poetry, Sketch 1," quoted by Boris M. Ejxenbaum in "The Theory of the Formal Method," *Readings in Russian Poetics: Formalist and Structuralist Views*, ed. Ladislav Matejka and Krystyna Pomorska (Cambridge, Mass.: MIT Press, 1971), p. 8.

15. See Viktor Sklovskij's seminal article "Art as Technique," *Russian Formalist Criticism. Four Essays* (Lincoln, Neb.: University of Nebraska Press, 1965), pp. 3–24. Herzberger has a different conception of the role of defamiliarization in Benet. See his article in *Revista de Estudios Hispánicos*, note 6 above.

16. Ejxenbaum, "Theory of the Formal Method," p. 30. See also Jurij Tynjanov's "On Literary Evolution," in *Readings in Russian Poetics*, pp. 66–78.

17. Ejxenbaum, "Theory of the Formal Method," p. 33.

18. "El arte literario es tan idóneo para hacer la revolución como el cuple patriótico para enardecer un país y para ganar una guerra en ultramar. Son cosas que rara vez se casan: la literatura por tener un 'status' propio, tiene su propio moral que no tiene por qué coincidir con el deber social, más general o más específico, impuesto por el momento histórico, tiene su propia constitución, su propia historia y—por así decirlo—sus clases dominantes y sus clases oprimidas, y por consiguiente, su propia revolución que llevar a cabo" ("Respuesta a Montero," p. 75).

## Janet Pérez: The Rhetoric of Ambiguity

1. Juan Benet, *La inspiración y el estilo*, 1st ed. (Madrid: Revista de Occidente, 1965; Barcelona: Seix Barral, 1973). All references are to the Seix Barral edition, with pagination given parenthetically in the text.

2. Kenneth Burke, *The Philosophy of Literary Form* (Baton Rouge: Louisiana State University Press, 1941), p. 321.

3. Kenneth Burke, *A Rhetoric of Motives* (Englewood Cliffs, N.J.: Prentice-Hall, 1950), pp. xiv, xv.

4. Ivor A. Richards, *The Philosophy of Rhetoric* (New York: Oxford University Press, 1936).

5. Ivor A. Richards, *Speculative Instruments* (Chicago: University of Chicago Press, 1955), p. 108.

6. Chaim Perelman, *The New Rhetoric*, trans. John Wilkinson and Purcell Weaver (South Bend, Ind.: University of Notre Dame Press, 1969).

7. Stephen Toulmin, *The Uses of Argument* (Cambridge: Cambridge University Press, 1958).

8. Marshall McLuhan, *Understanding Media: The Extensions of Man* (New York: McGraw-Hill, 1964). See particularly, "The Medium Is the Message," pp. 7–80.

*Esther W. Nelson: Narrative Perspective in "Volverás a Región"*

1. *The Metamorphosis of the Circle*, trans. Carley Dawson and Elliott Coleman (Baltimore, Md.: Johns Hopkins University Press, 1966), p. 189.
2. According to Gaston Bachelard, "Memory . . . does not record concrete duration, in the Bergsonian sense of the word. We are unable to relive duration that has been destroyed. We can only think of it in the line of an abstract time that is deprived of all thickness." *The Poetics of Space* (Boston: Beacon Press, 1964), p. 9.
3. Juan Benet, *Volverás a Región* (Barcelona: Ediciones Destino, 1967). All references are to this edition and are given in parentheses in the text.
4. David K. Herzberger has stated, "Much of Benet's style supports the notion that we are before the dream of reality instead of reality itself." "The Emergence of Juan Benet: A New Alternative for the Spanish Novel," *American Hispanist*, 1, no. 3 (November 1975), p. 10.
5. "Literalmente, la novela no comienza; su principio es una continuación, una respuesta a algo que ya se dijo o se pensó. La primera frase parece contestar a una observación sobre el paisaje novelesco, para afirmar, al menos inicialmente, su adscripción a una realidad concreta." Ricardo Gullón, "Una región laberíntica que bien pudiera llamarse España," *Insula*, no. 319 (June 1973) p. 10.
6. See Wayne Booth, *The Rhetoric of Fiction* (Chicago: University of Chicago Press, 1961), pp. 71–76, 160–61. It is important to distinguish between the implied author, whose existence is demanded by that of the literary reality, and the man Benet, who belongs to the real world. The real author may make mistakes, he may forget what he wrote, or even lose interest in maintaining the consistency with regard to story line, but the reader himself, as a result of a tendency to order reality logically, infers the existence of one whom he can presume does know the "whole story" and the accuracy of what is being transmitted by the narrator(s).
7. See Joseph Frank, "Spatial Form in Modern Literature," *Sewanee Review*, 53 (1945), pp. 221–40, 443–56, 643–53.
8. The same name is given to several characters, several names to a single character, and none at all to others. Even the "editor" makes little effort to clarify plot and claims to ignore the events between the death of María Timoner and the war: "Tal vez entre esos dos momentos no media otra cosa que la fuga" (p. 277). According to Manuel Durán: "Se diría que Benet quiere impedir a toda costa la identificación entre el lector y los personajes de su novela." "Juan Benet y la nueva novela española," *Cuadernos Americanos*, 195, no. 4 (1974), p. 201.

## Nelson R. Orringer: Epic in a Paralytic State: "Volverás a Región"

1. José Ortega y Gasset, ¿Qué es filosofía?, Obras Completas, 2d ed., 9 vols. (Madrid: Revista de Occidente, 1964), 8, p. 397.
2. Cf. Benet's interest in James Joyce. See Juan Benet, "Prólogo," to El 'Ulises' de James Joyce, by Stuart Gilbert, translated by Manuel de la Escalera (Madrid, 1971), mentioned in David K. Herzberger, The Novelistic World of Juan Benet (Clear Creek, Ind.: American Hispanist, 1976), p. 167.
3. José Ortega, "Estudios sobre la obra de Juan Benet," Cuadernos Hispanoamericanos, no. 284 (February 1974), p. 234.
4. Ibid., p. 233.
5. Juan Benet, "Epica, noética, poética . . .," Puerta de tierra (Barcelona: Seix Barral, 1970), p. 19. Subsequent citations to this work will be given in parentheses in the text.
6. "La entrada en la taberna," La inspiración y el estilo (Madrid: Revista de Occidente, 1965), p. 74. Henceforth all references to this work will appear in parentheses in the text.
7. Juan Benet, Volverás a Región (Barcelona: Ediciones Destino, 1967), p. 8. Henceforth all references to this work will appear in parentheses in the text.
8. Hermann Cohen, Asthetik des reinen Gefuhls (Berlin: Bruno Cassirer, 1912), 2, p. 18.
9. But Hernández, who lacks the impartiality of the true epic poet, actually makes himself a character of his epic as he harangues "gallegos de lluvia y calma,/catalanes de firmeza,/aragoneses de casta,/murcianos de dinamita,/frutalmente propagada,/leoneses, navarros, dueños/del hambre y el sudor y el hacha." "Vientos del pueblo me llevan," Antología (Buenos Aires: Losada, 1960), p. 84.
10. Cohen, Asthetik des reinen Gefuhls, p. 73; José Ortega y Gasset, Meditaciones del Quijote (Madrid: Revista de Occidente, 1957), p. 190.
11. On the Homeric gods, cf. C. M. Bowra, The Greek Experience (New York: Praeger, 1957), pp. 64–65.
12. Interview by Nelson R. Orringer, "Juan Benet a viva voz sobre la filosofía y ensayo actuales," Los Ensayistas, nos. 8–9 (March 1980), p. 63. Faulkner's phrase appears at the start of chapter 6 of Light in August.
13. In the interview by Antonio Núñez, "Encuentro con Juan Benet," Insula, no. 269 (April 1969), p. 4, Benet confesses the deep effect upon him of his experience of the Civil War when, at age nine, he found himself separated from his parents.
14. Herzberger, Novelistic World, p. 73.

## Stephen J. Summerhill: Prohibition and Transgression in "Volverás a Región" and "Una meditación"

1. Ricardo Gullón, "Una región laberíntica que bien pudiera llamarse España," Insula, no. 319 (June 1973), p. 10.

2. Marisa Martínez-Lázaro, "Juan Benet o la incertidumbre como fundamento," *El Urogallo*, nos. 11–12 (September-December, 1971), p. 176.

3. Antonio Núñez, "Encuentro con Juan Benet," *Insula*, no. 269 (April 1969), p. 4.

4. Quoted from Jorge Rodríguez Padrón, "Volviendo a Región," *Camp De L'Arpa*, no. 7 (August-September 1973), p. 38.

5. It is significant that the so-called objective narrator of *El Jarama* likewise introduces a "magical" or mythical element throughout the novel, particularly in the presentation of nature. See Darío Villanueva, *El Jarama de Sánchez Ferlosio: Su estructura y significado* (Santiago de Compostela: Universidad de Santiago de Compostela, 1973), pp. 135–49.

6. Juan Benet, *Volverás a Región* (Barcelona: Ediciones Destino, 1967), pp. 11–14. Further references to the novel will be from this edition and will be noted in parentheses in the text.

7. Manuel Durán, "Juan Benet y la nueva novela española," *Cuadernos Americanos*, 195, no. 4 (July-August 1974), p. 202.

8. The most obvious example is Coronel Gamallo, whose restrictive upbringing is described on pp. 71–72.

9. This child is discussed perceptively by José Ortega in "La dimensión temporal en *Volverás a Región* de Juan Benet," *Ensayos de la novela española moderna* by José Ortega (Madrid: José Porrúa Turanzas, 1974), p. 148.

10. Juan Benet, "Breve historia de *Volverás a Región*," *Revista de Occidente*, n.s. no. 134 (May 1974), p. 160.

11. One understands Freud as "perpetuating" myth in the sense suggested by Claude Lévi-Strauss, *Anthropologie Structurale* (Paris: Plon, 1958), p. 240, when he says that the Viennese psychoanalyst is as much a source of the myth of Oedipus as is Sophocles, insofar as he gives another version of it and contributes to our perception of it as a form of truth. The relationship between Freud and Benet has been seen by Alberto Oliart, "Viaje a Región," *Revista de Occidente*, n.s. no. 80 (November 1969), p. 232.

12. See the perceptive discussion of the novel in David K. Herzberger, *The Novelistic World of Juan Benet* (Clear Creek, Ind.: American Hispanist, 1976), pp. 43–69.

13. Núñez, "Encuentro con Juan Benet," p. 4.

14. The leitmotiv of the sacrifice, reiterated throughout the novel, is elaborately explained by Tío Ricardo, whose discussion utilized the Abraham-Isaac emblem, and thereby recalls Kierkegaard's meditations on the same topic in *Fear and Trembling*. It would be interesting to compare the two in order to detect a possible irony in the manipulation of the Danish writer's ideas.

15. Juan Benet, *Una meditación* (Barcelona: Seix Barral, 1970), pp. 211–14. Further references to this novel will be from this edition and will be noted in parentheses in the text.

16. For an excellent discussion of naturalization or conventionalization, see Jonathan Culler, *Structuralist Poetics: Structuralism, Linguistics and*

*the Study of Literature* (London: Routledge & Kegan Paul, 1975), pp. 131–60.

17. This, of course, is how both novels have been read by most critics and, indeed, many passages of each suggest that Región is a microcosm of Spain.

18. See Benet's discussion of style in *La inspiración y el estilo* (Madrid: Revista de Occidente, 1965), especially pp. 137–60. In this context, it is noteworthy that Benet sees the language of Spanish literature as formed by a historical fear of writers to *transgress* the canons of classical Spanish literature. Even at the level of style, then, the dialectic between prohibition and transgression permeates his thinking.

19. This distinction between pure form and pure meaning is admittedly abstract since actual texts are always meaningful form without ever being completely so, as Culler, *Structuralist Poetics*, p. 194, well shows. The point about Benet is the seeming deliberateness with which he adopts the position.

20. "[L'oeuvre littéraire] est, si l'on veut, du sens *suspendu*: elle s'offre en effet au lecteur comme un système signifiant déclaré mais se dérobe à lui comme objet signifié. Cette sorte de *de-ception*, de dé-prise du sens explique d'une part que l'oeuvre littéraire ait tant de force pour poser des questions au monde (en ébranlant les sens assurés que les croyances, idéologies et le sens commun semblent détenir), sans cependant jamais y répondre." "Qu'est-ce que la critique?" *Essais critiques* (Paris: Seuil, 1964), p. 256.

## Mary S. Vásquez: *The Creative Task: Existential Self-Invention in "Una meditación"*

1. Gonzalo Sobejano, *Novela española de nuestro tiempo*, 2d ed. (Madrid: Prensa Española, 1975), p. 564.

2. Juan Benet, *Una meditación* (Barcelona: Seix Barral, 1970), p. 67. All further quotes from *Una meditación* are from the same edition and will be given in parentheses in the text.

3. David K. Herzberger discusses the use of oxymoronic descriptions in several Benet novels in his "The Emergence of Juan Benet: A New Alternative for the Spanish Novel," *American Hispanist*, 1, no. 3 (November 1975), pp. 6–12. Herzberger's studies (see also his *The Novelistic World of Juan Benet*, [Clear Creek, Ind.: American Hispanist, 1976]) and the Sobejano chapter (see n. 1 above) are two of the very few substantive examinations of *Una meditación*.

## Julia Lupinacci Wescott: *Subversion of Character Conventions in Benet's Trilogy*

1. E. H. Gombrich, *Art and Illusion* (Princeton, N.J.: Princeton University Press, 1972), p. 281.

2. See, for example, W. J. Harvey, *Character and the Novel* (Ithaca, N.Y.:

Cornell University Press, 1968), p. 23; Fernando Ferrara, "Theory and Model for the Structural Analysis of Fiction," *New Literary History*, 5 (1974), pp. 245–68; Seymour Chatman, *Story and Discourse: Narrative Structure in Fiction and Film* (Ithaca, N.Y.: Cornell University Press, 1978), p. 125.

3. Roland Barthes, in *S/Z* (New York: Hill and Wang, 1974), p. 4, defines this term as "a classic text." It denotes what we might call a "traditional" novel.

4. The trilogy comprises *Volverás a Región* (Barcelona: Ediciones Destino, 1967); *Una meditación* (Barcelona: Seix Barral, 1970); and *Un viaje de invierno* (Barcelona: La Gaya Ciencia, 1972).

5. John Bayley, "Character and Consciousness," *New Literary History*, 5 (1974), p. 234.

6. Oswald Ducrot and Tzvetan Todorov, "Character," *Encyclopedic Dictionary of the Sciences of Language*, trans. Catherine Porter (Baltimore, Md.: Johns Hopkins University Press, 1979), p. 222.

7. E. M. Forster, *Aspects of the Novel* (New York: Harcourt Brace and Co., 1927), p. 74.

8. Bayley, "Character and Consciousness," p. 229.

9. Gonzalo Sobejano describes them as "desdibujados" in *Novela española de nuestro tiempo*, 2d ed. (Madrid: Prensa Española, 1975), p. 573.

10. José Ortega has also noted this but without comment on the effect produced. See "Estudios sobre la obra de Juan Benet," *Cuadernos Hispanoamericanos*, no. 284 (February 1974), p. 232.

11. *Volverás a Región* (Madrid: Alianza, 1974), p. 20. Hereafter, all references are to this edition and will appear in the text.

12. Chatman, *Story and Discourse*, p. 131.

13. G. W. Allport, "What Is a Trait of Personality?" *Journal of Abnormal and Social Psychology*, 25 (1931), p. 368; quoted in Chatman, *Story and Discourse*, p. 122.

14. Ortega terms it "un diálogo que se nutre fundamentalmente de los soliloquios de ambos." "Estudios sobre la obra de Juan Benet," p. 232. David K. Herzberger defines it as a "complex framework of third-person narrator and pseudo-dialogues between the two principal characters" (*The Novelistic World of Juan Benet* [Clear Creek, Ind.: American Hispanist, 1976], p. 43), and later as "monologues" (p. 66).

15. José Ortega expresses no doubt that the two protagonists "mantienen un diálogo que en realidad es soliloquio más que monólogo interior, pues en el caso de estos personajes existe comunicación, mientras que en el monólogo interior es proceso psíquico." See *Ensayos de la novela española moderna* (Madrid: Ediciones José Porrúa Turanzas, 1974), p. 147.

16. Dorrit Cohn, *Transparent Minds: Narrative Modes for Presenting Consciousness in Fiction* (Princeton, N.J.: Princeton University Press, 1978), p. 143.

17. Ibid., pp. 184–86, 247–55.

18. David K. Herzberger also points to narrational undercutting in "The Emergence of Juan Benet: A New Alternative for the Spanish Novel," *American Hispanist*, 1, no. 3 (November 1975), p. 10.

19. *Una meditación* (Barcelona: Seix Barral, 1970), p. 7. Hereafter, all references to *Una meditación* are to this edition and will appear in the text.
20. Ortega, in contrast, sees memory as rejecting reasoning. See "Estudios sobre la obra de Juan Benet," p. 244.
21. *Un viaje de invierno* (Barcelona: La Gaya Ciencia, 1972), p. 9. Hereafter all references to *Un viaje de invierno* are to this edition and will appear in the text.
22. Cohn, *Transparent Minds*, p. 31.
23. See, for example, Herzberger, *Novelistic World of Juan Benet*, p. 115, who refers to his concurrence with José Domingo, "Los caminos de la experimentación: Torrente Ballester, Benet," *Insula*, no. 312 (November 1972), p. 6.
24. Cohn, *Transparent Minds*, p. 29.
25. Darío Villanueva also makes this point in "La novela de Juan Benet," *Camp de l'Arpa*, no. 8 (November 1973), p. 14.
26. I would contest the fundamental premise, then, of Teresa Aveleyra's "Algo sobre las criaturas de Juan Benet," *Nueva Revista de Filología Hispánica*, 23, no. 1 (1974), pp. 121–30.
27. For an interesting article on this subject, see Félix Martínez-Bonati, "Representation and Fiction," *Dispositio*, 5, nos. 13–14 (1980), pp. 19–33.
28. Chatman, *Story and Discourse*, p. 125.

## Gonzalo Díaz-Migoyo: Reading/Writing Ironies in "En el estado"

1. As Félix de Azúa has pointed out in "El texto invisible," *Los Cuadernos de la Gaya Ciencia*, 1 (Barcelona, 1975), pp. 9–21.
2. In his interview with J. A. Hernández, "Juan Benet, 1976," *MLN*, 92 (1977), p. 348.
3. Remarks made during "coloquios" at Coloquio Sobre Novela Española Actual at Fundación Juan March, 2–7 June 1975, in *Novela española actual*, edited by Andrés Amorós (Madrid: Fundación Juan March/Editorial Cátedra, 1977), p. 178.
4. For a fuller development see my "El funcionamiento de la ironía," *Espiral/Revista* 7 (Madrid, 1980), pp. 45–68.
5. Juan Benet, *En el estado* (Madrid: Alfaguara, 1977). Future references to *En el estado* are to this edition and appear in the text.
6. The devoted reader of Benet, ready to imitate Joan of Arc and her voices, would be delighted to recognize these words once again on page 82 of his 1980 novel, *Saúl ante Samuel* (Barcelona: La Gaya Ciencia): "Se había curvado el cuadro de la historia para situarlos al fondo de un salón, en el momento en que cantaran 'O Richard, o mon roi.'"
7. I realize that it does not help matters to point out that the lady's orgasms are the same in number as Benet's novels up to 1977; and that therefore the sixth orgasm she dreads may stand for *En el estado* itself! The consequences of this kind of twisted allegorical (or is it symbolic?) reading are mindboggling. At any rate, there is a precedent in Leopoldo Azancot's review of *En el estado*, "Juan Benet ante el reto de la democracia," *Infor-*

*maciones de las Artes y las Letras* (supplement to *Informaciones* [Madrid]
no. 475 (25 August 1977), p. 3.
   8. Juan Benet, *La inspiración y el estilo* (Madrid: Revista de Occidente,
1966), p. 107.

*David K. Herzberger: The Theme of Warring Brothers in "Saúl*
*ante Samuel"*

   1. G. R. Strange, Introduction to William Makepeace Thackeray, *The*
*History of Henry Edmond, Esq.* (New York: Holt, Rinehart & Winston,
1962), p. xv.
   2. Juan Benet, *Una meditación* (Barcelona: Seix Barral, 1970), p. 63.
   3. For Benet's most important essay on the Spanish Civil War and the
tragic consequences of its outcome, see his ¿*Qué fue la guerra civil?* (Barcelona: La Gaya Ciencia, 1976).
   4. Juan Benet, *Saúl ante Samuel* (Barcelona: La Gaya Ciencia, 1980), p.
330. Future references to *Saúl ante Samuel* are to this edition and are noted
in the text.
   5. For an overview of the Cain/Abel theme in literature, as well as its
various biblical interpretations, see Honor Matthews, *The Primal Curse*
(New York: Schocken Books, 1967); and chapter 1 of Lorraine Keilstrup,
"The Myth of Cain in the Early English Drama," Ph.D. diss., University of
Nebraska, 1974.

*Randolph D. Pope: Benet, Faulkner, and Bergson's Memory*

   1. "De Canudos a Macondo," *Revista de Occidente*, n.s. no. 70 (January
1969), p. 52.
   2. In one of the first and best studies of *Volverás a Región*, written by
Alberto Oliart, *Revista de Occidente*, n.s. no. 80 (1969), 224–34, the influence of Faulkner and Kafka is noted briefly on p. 230. Edenia Guillermo
and Juana Amelia Hernández in *La novelística española de los 60* (New
York: Eliseo Torres, 1971), p. 149, limit their comments to saying that the
influence of Faulkner is evident in all of Benet's work. Santos Sanz Villanueva in *Historia de la novela social española (1942–75)* (Madrid: Al-
hambra, 1980), p. 129, remarks that Faulkner is "very present" in Benet's
novels.
   3. The references in this paragraph, when they are to a specific work, are
the following: Angel Rama, *Rubén Darío y el Modernismo* (*Circunstancia*
*socioeconómica de un arte americano*) (Caracas: Universidad de Venez-
uela, 1970); Hans Robert Jauss, *Literaturgeschichte als Provokation* (Frank-
furt am Main: Suhrkamp, 1970); Jonathan Culler, *Structuralist Poetics*
(Ithaca, N.Y.: Cornell University Press, 1975), who defines structuralist poetics as "the theory of the practice of reading" (p. 259); Harold Bloom,
*The Anxiety of Influence* (London: Oxford University Press, 1973); W.
Jackson Bate, *The Burden of the Past and the English Poet* (Cambridge,
Mass.: Harvard University Press, 1970); Manuel Pedro González, *Colo-*

*quio de la novela hispanoamericana* (Mexico: Fondo de Cultura Económica, 1967); Rene Wellek, "The Concept of Evolution in Literary Theory," *Concepts of Criticism* (New Haven, Conn.: Yale University Press, 1977), and Erich Koehler in a lecture at the University of Freiburg in July of 1971, where his suggestions that there existed a relative independence of literary history from the socioeconomical base were received with an uproar of protest from most of the students present.

4. Santos Sanz Villanueva, in his *Historia de la novela social española*, p. 222, regards the reception of Benet's works as "sintomática" because "la manera en que están escritas estas novelas no cambia mucho después de las dos primeras, pero su aceptación, sí." In the prologue to the second edition of *Volverás a Región* (Madrid: Alianza Editorial, 1974), Benet tells about the vicissitudes of trying to find an editor. Quotes in the present study will be from this edition of the novel.

5. The most detailed and precise analysis of this aspect has been done by David K. Herzberger, *The Novelistic World of Juan Benet* (Clear Creek, Ind.: American Hispanist, 1976). For the influence of Faulkner on Lino Novás Calvo, Onetti, José Revueltas, and Juan Rulfo, see James E. Irby's *La influencia de William Faulkner en cuatro narradores hispanoamericanos* (Mexico: Universidad Nacional Autónoma de México, 1956).

6. *Volverás a Región*, p. 74. During a colloquium organized by the Fundación Juan March, published later under the title *Novela española actual* (Madrid: Fundación Juan March/Editorial Cátedra, 1976), Benet was asked if Región should be interpreted as a compendium or abbreviation for Spain. He answered: "No sé si tal correspondencia existe" (p. 185).

7. Robert C. Spires has studied the mythical structure of *Volverás a Región* in *La novela española de posguerra* (Madrid: Cupsa Editorial, 1978), pp. 237–44. For Faulkner's use of myth, see Walter Brylowski's *Faulkner's Olympian Laugh, Myth in the Novels* (Detroit, Mich.: Wayne State University Press, 1968). In *Faulkner at Nagano,* ed. Robert A. Jelliffe (Tokyo, 1956), p. 45, Faulkner states: "To me the Old Testament is some of the finest, most robust and most amusing folklore I know." For Benet's study of the style of the Bible, see *La inspiración y el estilo* (Barcelona: Seix Barral, 1973), pp. 45–54.

8. *Faulkner at the University*, edited by Frederick L. Gwynn and Joseph L. Blotner (Charlottesville: University of Virginia Press, 1957), pp. 273–74; the best study of Benet's contradictions, ambiguities, and riddles is David K. Herzberger's "Enigma as Narrative Determinant in the Novels of Juan Benet," *Hispanic Review*, 47 (1979), pp. 149–57. The doctor in *Volverás a Región* states about the story of his father: "yo no sabré nunca de fijo el verdadero desenlace" (p. 120), and his interlocutor says: "Ha pasado tanto tiempo y ha sido tal mi soledad que he llegado a dudar si todo aquello ocurrió como lo he dicho" (pp. 278–79); in *Saúl ante Samuel* one reads: "a la postre toda historia resulta oscura, con un origen indefinido y un haz de metamorfoseantes intenciones que arrojarán una resultante imprevisible" (p. 128).

9. For examples of extended meditations see pp. 90–91 of *Volverás a*

*Región*; pp. 29–34 of *Una meditación* (Barcelona: Seix Barral, 1970); and p. 143 of William Faulkner, *Absalom, Absalom* (New York: The Modern Library, 1936).

10. During an interesting conversation with Nelson R. Orringer, "Juan Benet a viva voz sobre la filosofía y el ensayo actuales," *Los Ensayistas*, nos. 8–9 (March 1980), pp. 59–65, Benet admits that Bergson, whose works he read in their entirety, exerted the greatest influence on him. On the importance of Bergson for Faulkner, see the chapter that Cleanth Brooks dedicates to this question in *William Faulkner, Toward Yoknapatawpha and Beyond* (New Haven, Conn.: Yale University Press, 1978), pp. 251–82.

11. Henri Bergson, *L'Evolution créatrice, Oeuvres* (Paris: Presses Universitaires de France, 1959), p. 498. All translations from French texts are my own.

12. Henri Bergson, *Matière et mémoire, Oeuvres*, pp. 183 and 213.

13. *Volverás a Región*, p. 23. While speaking to Orringer, Benet remembers a sentence by Faulkner, from *Light in August*, "that for someone who writes about this theme is nothing less than Einstein's law of memory: at the beginning of Chapter 6 it says: 'Memory believes before knowledge remembers'" ("Juan Benet a viva voz," p. 63).

14. William Faulkner, *Absalom, Absalom*, p. 261. In *Go Down, Moses* (New York: Modern Library, 1955), p. 326, Faulkner writes: "memory at least does last." In *Faulkner at the University*, Faulkner remarks: "No man is himself, he's the sum of his past" (p. 48).

15. *Un viaje de invierno* (Barcelona: La Gaya Ciencia, 1972), p. 226.

16. William Faulkner, *The Sound and the Fury* (New York: Vintage Books, 1929), p. 104; Faulkner, *Absalom, Absalom*, p. 18.

17. William Faulkner, *Lion in the Garden*, ed. James Merriwether and Michael Millgate (New York: Random House, 1968), p. 70.

18. Richard P. Adams, in *Faulkner, Myth and Motion* (Princeton, N.J.: Princeton University Press, 1968), p. 225, writes: "Each of the Compson brothers . . . is a static obstacle to the motion of life."

19. In *Matière et mémoire* Bergson states: "Refined or coarse, any language implies many things that it can't express. Essentially discontinuous, because it must proceed by using juxtaposed words, words do no more than hint at long intervals the principal stages of the movement of thought" (*Oeuvres*, p. 269). For an attempt to refute Bergson's ideas about language, see Kamal Youssef El-Hage, *La Valeur du langage chez Henri Bergson* (Beirut: Publications de l'Universite Libanaise, 1971). Bergson affirms clearly: "thought overflows the limitations of language" (*Essai sur les données immédiates de la conscience, Oeuvres*, p. 109).

20. Bergson, *La Pensée et le mouvant, Oeuvres*, p. 1397.

21. *En ciernes* (Madrid: Taurus, 1976), p. 30.

22. In *Matière et mémoire*, Bergson draws an illustration to the text, in which all of the diverse and diverging levels of analysis are seen emerging from one starting point and forming an inverted cone above it, *Oeuvres*, p. 302.

23. Bergson, *L'Énergie spirituelle, Oeuvres*, p. 849.

24. Bergson, *Essai sur les données immédiates de la conscience, Oeuv-*

*res*, p. 122: "To tell the truth, the deeper states of our soul, those that translate themselves into free acts, express and encompass the totality of our past history."

25. Angel S. Harguíndez, "El último sudista," *El País Semanal*, 23 November 1980, p. 12.

## Roberto C. Manteiga: Time, Space, and Narration in Juan Benet's Short Stories

1. Prior to 1977 Benet had published several collections of short fiction under the titles *Nunca llegarás a nada* (1961), *Una tumba* (1971), *Cinco narraciones y dos fábulas* (1972), and *Sub rosa* (1973). In 1977 Benet collected all of the short fiction he had written to date and, with the exception of one short story the author says he would like to forget and a few fables that don't pertain to the genre, published them in a two-volume set by Alianza Editorial. The first volume, says the author, includes all of those narratives that take place in the mythical space of Región and the second volume, those that take place in any other space, mythical or otherwise. (This is true of all of the stories with the exception of "Después," which is included in volume two but obviously takes place in Región since the geographical place names and references to certain characters are the same as those in Benet's other stories and novels about Región.) Benet adds, sarcastically, that by sheer coincidence both volumes have exactly the same number of pages, which is not only a great advantage editorially speaking, but could possibly provide critics with yet another point of consideration

2. The problematic question of the nature of time and space is not a modern one by any means. We find studies on the relationship of time to space as far back as Aristotle's *Poetics*. There is no denying, however, that, with the recent interest in the study of narrative structures, the literary author's concern for (or preoccupation with) these elements has been paramount.

3. For other studies on time and space in Benet's works see in particular David K. Herzberger, *The Novelistic World of Juan Benet* (Clear Creek, Ind.: American Hispanist, 1976); Andrei Ionescu, "Explorarea unui spatiu mitic," *Seculol XX*, nos. 166–67 (1974), pp. 87–92; José Ortega, "La dimensión temporal en *Volverás a Región*," "*Una meditación* de Benet: Segunda variación sobre la ruina temporal," and "Razón, nostalgia y destino de *Un viaje de invierno*" in *Ensayos de la novela española moderna* (Madrid: José Porrúa Turanzas, 1974); Randolph D. Pope, "Benet, Faulkner, and Bergson's Memory," herein; Mary S. Vásquez, "Taking the Measure of the Past: Existential Self-Creation in Benet's *Una meditación*" (Paper presented at Rocky Mountain Modern Language Association Convention, Albuquerque, N. Mex., October 1979).

4. There are a few stories presented according to linear time in which the reader can follow the story line from beginning to end.

5. See Henri Bergson, *Time and Free Will*, trans. by F. L. Pogson (London: George Allen and Unwin, 1910).

6. See Henri Bergson, *Matter and Memory*, trans. Nancy Margaret Paul and W. Scott Palmer (New York: Macmillan, 1911).

7. See Margaret Church, *Time and Reality* (Chapel Hill, N.C.: University of North Carolina Press, 1949).

8. *Writers at Work: The Paris Review Interviews*, ed. Malcolm Cowley (New York: Viking Press, 1959), p. 141.

9. Loic Bouvard, "Conversations with William Faulkner," *Modern Fiction Studies* (Winter 1959–60), p. 362.

10. Patricia Drechsel Tobin, *Time and the Novel, The Genealogical Imperative* (Princeton, N.J.: Princeton University Press, 1978), p. 112.

11. See Juan Benet, *Un viaje de invierno* (Madrid: Cátedra, 1980).

12. Sharon Spencer, *Time and Structure in the Modern Novel* (New York: New York University Press, 1971), p. 151. Of particular importance is part III, in which Spencer discusses the spatialization of time.

13. Seymour Chatman, *Story and Discourse: Narrative Structure in Fiction and Film* (Ithaca, N.Y.: Cornell University Press, 1978), p. 197.

14. Ibid., p. 204

15. Chatman defines unreliable narration as the presence of an implied author carrying on a secret communication with an implied reader at variance with the actual words he uses and at the expense of the narrator, who is the victim or "butt" (p. 229). Chatman's theory does not allow for the possibility of an unreliable covert narrator. It should also be pointed out that while most of Benet's short stories have only one narrator, multiple narration is not uncommon. The technique of employing several often contradictory narrators helps to create an enigmatic picture of reality that the author consciously strives to present in his work.

16. Herzberger, *Novelistic World of Juan Benet*, p. 49.

17. Ibid., p. 21.

18. Ibid., p. 85

19. See ibid., p. 106, for Herzberger's account of the Brigadier's death.

20. The boy, Benet tells us, is fascinated upon seeing his own footprints at the bottom of the grave. In them he is able to decipher a hidden meaning: "Como si se tratara de una leyenda en una de esas escrituras cúficas de un solo símbolo de cuyas diferentes posiciones en el plano es preciso derivar el significado." Juan Benet, *Cuentos completos*, 2 vols. (Madrid: Alianza Editorial, 1977), vol. 1, p. 16. Subsequent quotes from this work will be given by the volume and page number in the text.

21. If the narrator here is indirectly expressing the thoughts of his character rather than philosophizing on his own he is, in fact, acting as covert narrator, which I discussed earlier.

22. There are a series of descriptive motifs associated with the character Don Lucas, including a wide-brimmed felt hat, white boots, and a cigarette holder. We are able to identify him later as Rosa's killer through the narrator's reference to "las botas blancas junto a su cabeza."

23. A phrase used by Jorge Luis Borges in defining "El Aleph." The narrator here makes an allusion to a frustrated courtship concluded in that very same year, 1915, and proceeds to describe a scene in which Don Lucas surprises his lover in bed with someone else.

24. The most likely possibility is that César is actually Queiles's son and that Queiles's stepdaughter is, in fact, the daughter of Honorio Abrantes. Honorio's wife, who is the richest woman in the county, had an affair with someone who remains unnamed. César is the illegitimate fruit of that relationship, and his mother makes him sole inheritor of her estate. Honorio plottingly tries to use what he knows of his wife's adulterous activities in order to get her possessions. Knowing that César will not live to inherit the money—César had been born sickly and not given long to live—Honorio acknowledges legally but secretly that the child is not his but Queiles's. Queiles's stepdaughter, in the meantime, turns out to be the illegitimate child of Honorio Abrantes and la señorita Ferdinandi. A short time after her affair with Honorio la señorita Ferdinandi married Queiles and later died giving birth to Honorio's child. Honorio is quick to acknowledge that this child is his daughter, knowing that upon her death and with Queiles out of the way he will inherit Montranza, the tract of land he so much desired.

25. I use Chatman's term "narratee" because the reader is left with the impression that the narrator is talking to someone specific, although that someone is never identified.

26. Pedro Ramírez Molas, *Tiempo y narración* (Madrid: Gredos, 1978), p. 81.

27. Ibid.

28. Ibid., p. 52. This concept, which I refer to as "frozen time," is apparent in a number of Benet's works. Perhaps the most familiar example is the child in *Volverás a Región*, who becomes trapped in that moment when he imagines that he hears the return of the car that had taken his mother away.

29. "Catálisis," says Benet, is a chemical reaction between two bodies after which the bodies appear unaltered.

COMPILED BY MALCOLM ALAN COMPITELLO

# Bibliography

*Works by Juan Benet (arranged chronologically under each heading)*

## NOVELS AND SHORT FICTION

*Nunca llegarás a nada.* Madrid: Editorial Tebas, 1961; Reprint. Madrid: Alianza Editorial, 1969.
*Volverás a Región.* Barcelona: Ediciones Destino, 1967; 2d ed. Madrid: Alianza Editorial, 1974.
"La violencia de la posguerra." *Revista de Occidente*, n.s., no. 81 (December 1969), pp. 348–61. (Fragment of *Una meditación*).
*Una meditación.* Barcelona: Seix Barral, 1970.
"Los padres." *El Urogallo*, no. 1 (February 1970), pp. 62–66.
*Una tumba.* Barcelona: Lumen, 1971.
*5 narraciones y 2 fábulas.* Barcelona: La Gaya Ciencia, 1972.
*Un viaje de invierno.* Barcelona: La Gaya Ciencia, 1972.
*La otra casa de Mazón.* Barcelona: Seix Barral, 1973.
*Sub rosa.* Barcelona: La Gaya Ciencia, 1973.
"Horas en apariencia vacías." *Plural: Revista Mensual de Excelsior*, no. 25 (October 1973), pp. 20–24.
"*Amor vacui.*" *Plural*, no. 41 (February 1975).
"Syllabus." In *Cuentos Españoles Concertados. De Clarín a Benet.* Edited by Gonzalo Sobejano and Gary D. Keller. New York: Harcourt Brace Jovanovich, 1975, pp. 256–62. (Originally appeared in *5 narraciones y 2 fábulas.*)
"Retazo." In *Cuaderno de Norte. Norte: Revista Hispánica de Amsterdam*, 1976, pp. 79–82. (Fragment of an unpublished novel).
*Cuentos completos.* 2 vols. Madrid: Alianza Editorial, 1977.
*En el estado.* Madrid: Alfaguara, 1977.
"Un tema de otro tiempo." *Vuelta* (Mexico City), no. 2 (January 1977), pp. 4–7. (Chapter of *En el estado*).

153

*Del pozo y del Numa: Un ensayo y una leyenda*. Barcelona: La Gaya Ciencia, 1978.

"Una leyenda: Numa." *Del pozo y del Numa: Un ensayo y una leyenda*. Barcelona: La Gaya Ciencia, 1978, pp. 96–168.

"Un fragmento." In *Nueva Estafeta*, no. 2 (January 1979), pp. 8–14.

*El aire de un crimen*. Barcelona: Planeta, 1980.

*Saúl ante Samuel*. Barcelona: La Gaya Ciencia, 1980.

*Un viaje de invierno*. Edited by Diego Martínez Torrón. Madrid: Cátedra, 1980.

"*Trece fábulas y media*." *El País* (Madrid) *Suplemento Literario*, no. 82 (17 May 1981), p. 7. (Prepublication fragments of book by same name).

*Trece fábulas y media*. Madrid: Alfaguara, 1981.

*Una tumba y otros relatos*. Edited by Ricardo Gullón. Madrid: Taurus, 1981.

*A Meditation*: Translated by Gregory Rabassa. New York: Persea Books, 1982.

THEATER

*Max. Revista Española*, no. 4 (November-December 1953), pp. 409–30.

*Agonía confutans. Cuadernos Hispanoamericanos*, no. 236 (August 1969), pp. 307–21.

*Teatro*. Madrid: Siglo XXI de España, 1970. (Contains *Anastas o el origen de la constitución*, *Agonía confutans*, and *Un caso de conciencia*).

POETRY

"Dos poemas: 'En cauria,' 'Un enigma.'" *El Urogallo*, no. 19 (September 1972), pp. 7–8.

TRANSLATIONS

*A este lado del Paraíso*. Translation of *This Side of Paradise*, by F. Scott Fitzgerald. Madrid: Alianza Editorial, 1968.

ESSAYS

*La inspiración y el estilo*. Madrid: Revista de Occidente, 1965. Reprint. Barcelona: Seix Barral, 1973.

*Puerta de tierra*. Barcelona: Seix Barral, 1970.

*El ángel del Señor abandona a Tobías*. Barcelona: La Gaya Ciencia, 1976.

*En ciernes*. Madrid: Taurus, 1976.

*¿Qué fue la guerra civil?* Barcelona: La Gaya Ciencia, 1976.

"Un ensayo: La deuda de la novela hacia el poema religioso de la antigüedad." *Del pozo y del Numa: Un ensayo y una leyenda*. Barcelona: La Gaya Ciencia, 1978, pp. 9–95.

Benet, Juan. *La moviola de Eurípides*. Madrid: Taurus, 1982.

ARTICLES AND BOOK REVIEWS

"Baroja y la disgregación de la novela." *Indice de Artes y Letras*, nos. 71–72 (December-January 1953–54). Reprint. *Indice*, nos. 301–302 (January-February 1972), p. 42.

"Joseph Heller: Trampa 22." Review of *Catch 22*. *Revista de Occidente*, n.s. no. 2 (May 1963), pp. 247–50.
"Agonía del humor." *Revista de Occidente*, n.s. no. ll (February 1964), pp. 235–41.
"Francisco Candel: *Los otros catalanes*." Book review. *Revista de Occidente*, n.s. no. 34 (January 1966), pp. 117–22.
"Ilusitania." *Revista de Occidente*, n.s. no. 54 (September 1967), pp. 336–52.
"Toledo sitiado." *Cuadernos Hispanoamericanos*, no. 216 (December 1967), pp. 571–81.
"De Canudos a Macondo." *Revista de Occidente*, n.s. no. 70 (January 1969), pp. 49–57.
"Cordelia Khan." *Cuadernos Hispanoamericanos*, no. 231 (March 1969), pp. 503–21. Reprint. *Puerta de tierra*. Barcelona: Seix Barral, 1970, pp. 142–67.
"Cinco respuestas a Proust." *Informaciones de las Artes y las Letras* (supplement to *Informaciones* [Madrid]), 10 July 1969, p. 3.
"Samuel Beckett, Premio Nobel, 1969." *Revista de Occidente*, n.s. no. 83 (February 1970), pp. 226–30.
"Contra James Joyce." *Informaciones de las Artes y las Letras* (supplement to *Informaciones* [Madrid]), 9 July 1970, pp. 1–2.
"Mesa redonda sobre la novela." *Cuadernos para el Diálogo*, special issue, 23 (December 1970), pp. 45–52.
"Reflexiones sobre Galdós." *Cuadernos para el Diálogo*, special issue, 23 (December 1970), pp. 13–15.
"Respuesta al señor Montero." *Cuadernos para el Diálogo*, special issue, 23 (December 1970), pp. 75–76.
"Prólogo" to *Industrias y andanzas de Alfanhuí*, by Rafael Sánchez Ferlosio. Barcelona: Salvat, 1970, pp. 11–15.
"Prólogo" to *Las palmeras salvajes*, by William Faulkner. Translated by Jorge Luis Borges. Barcelona: E.D.H.A.S.A., 1970, pp. 7–16.
"Prólogo" to *Benito Cereno*, by Herman Melville. Madrid: RTV, Salvat, 1970, pp. 5–11.
"Prólogo" to *El 'Ulises' de James Joyce*, by Stuart Gilbert. Translated by Manuel de la Escalera. Madrid: Siglo XXI de España, 1971, pp. 1–24.
"Los escritores y la edición del libro." *Cuadernos para el Diálogo*, no. 96 (August 1971), pp. 24–25.
"U.S.A.: *Babilonia revisitado*." *Triunfo*, no. 301 (1972), p. 41.
"La esferodoxia." *Cuadernos para el Diálogo*, no. 100 (January 1972), pp. 102–3.
"El crítico, hombre del orden." *Cuadernos para el Diálogo*, nos. 301–302 (January-February 1972), pp. 41–42.
"Barojiana." In *Barojiana*, by Juan Benet et al. Madrid: Taurus, 1972, pp. 11–45.
"Breve historia de *Volverás a Región*." Revista de Occidente, n.s. no. 134 (May 1974), pp. 160–65. (Also appears as "Prólogo a la segunda edición," in the Alianza Editorial edition of *Volverás a Región*, pp. 7–11).

"From Madrid, Observations on Military Behavior." Translated by Barbara Solomon. *New York Times*, 15 August 1975, p. 35.

"Dionisio Ridruejo." *Litoral*, nos. 51–52 (1975), p. 119.

"Introducción" to *Cría cuervos*, by Carlos Saura. Madrid: Elias Querejeta Ediciones, 1975, pp. 9–16.

"El hermano Solzhenitsyn." *Cuadernos para el Diálogo*, n.s. no. 157 (27 March 1976), p. 26.

"¿ Se sentó la duquesa a la derecha de don Quijote?" *Los Cuadernos de la Gaya Ciencia*, no. 3 (March 1976), pp. 7–31. Reprint. *En ciernes*. Madrid: Taurus, 1976, pp. 11–41.

"La fisiología del pasillo." *El País Semanal* (Madrid), no. 27 (3 April 1977), p. 3.

"La fisiología del pasillo." *El País Semanal* (Madrid), no. 28 (10 April 1977), p. 3.

"La fisiología del pasillo." *El País Semanal* (Madrid), n.s. no. 1 (17 April 1977), p. 39.

"Prólogo" to *Cuentos completos*, by Juan Benet, vol. 1. Madrid: Alianza Editorial, 1977, pp. 7–9.

"Valedictoria a Dionisio." *Dionisio Ridruejo de la falange a la oposición*, by Juan Benet et al. Madrid: Taurus, 1977, pp. 11–20.

"A Short Biographia Literaria." Lecture read for BBC, London. 20 August 1977. Published in *La moviola de Eurípides*. Madrid: Taurus, 1982, pp. 59–75.

"Tribuna libre: Proyecto para una constitución." *El País* (Madrid), 4 July 1978, p. 9.

"Onda y corpúsculo en el *Quijote*." Lecture read at Harvard University. 26 April 1979. Published in an expanded version in *La moviola de Eurípides*. Madrid: Taurus, 1982, pp. 77–115.

"El Tizón." *El País* (Madrid), 3 August 1980, p. 9.

"La esencia sigue igual." *Cambio 16*, no. 470 (1 December 1980), p. 176.

"Consideraciones sobre el hipérbaton." *Revista de Occidente*. 3d series, 6 (July-December 1981), pp. 27–39. Reprint. *La moviola de Eurípides*. Madrid: Taurus, 1982, pp. 54–58.

"Segunda propuesta al gobierno." *El País* (Madrid), 3 November 1981, pp. 11–12.

INTERVIEWS/ANSWERS TO ENCUESTAS/ADDRESSES

Interview by Miguel Fernández-Braso: "Juan Benet: un talento excitado." *Pueblo* (12 March 1969). Reprint. Miguel Fernández-Braso, *De escritor a escritor*. Barcelona: Taber, 1970, pp. 197–203.

Interview by Antonio Núñez. "Encuentro con Juan Benet." *Insula*, no. 269 (April 1969), p. 4.

Answers to "Encuesta II. Novela." *Cuadernos para el Diálogo*, special issue, 14 (May 1969), p. 68.

Interview by Juan Pedro Quiñonero. "Juan Benet: entre la ironía y la destrucción." *Informaciones de las Artes y las Letras* (Supplement to *Informaciones* [Madrid]), 2 August 1969, p. 3.

Interview by Eduardo García Rico: "Juan Benet: Joyce es de segunda fila." *Triunfo*, no. 249 (22 August 1970), p. 2.

Interview by Fernando Tola de Habich and Patricia Grieve. In *Los españoles y el boom*, by Fernando Tola de Habich and Patricia Grieve. Caracas: Editorial Tiempo Nuevo, 1971, pp. 25–41.

Interview by Federico Campbell. "Juan Benet o el azar." In *Infame turba*, by Federico Campbell. Barcelona: Lumen, 1971, pp. 293–310.

Answer to *encuesta* on social literature in Spain. In *Literatura y política. En torno al realismo español*, by Eduardo García Rico. Colección Los Suplementos, no. 19. Madrid: *Cuadernos para el Diálogo*, 1971, p. 19.

Answers to *encuesta* on literature and education in Spain. In *Literatura y educación*, edited by Fernando Lázaro Carreter. Madrid: Castalia, 1974, pp. 197–206.

Remarks made to Radio Televisión Española, 3 February 1975. (To my knowledge unpublished).

Remarks made during "Coloquios" at Coloquio sobre Novela Española Actual at Fundación Juan March, 2–7 June 1975. *Novela española actual*, edited by Andrés Amorós. Madrid: Fundación Juan March/Editorial Cátedra, 1977.

"Respuestas de Juan Benet a un cuestionario mínimo." *Cuaderno de Norte. Norte: Revista Hispánica de Amsterdam.* Special issue devoted to Agusto Roa Bastos and Juan Benet, 1976, pp. 76–78.

Interview by José Hernández. "Juan Benet, 1976." *MLN*, 92 (1977), pp. 346–55.

Answers to *encuesta* by Ismael Fuente Lafuente. "Benet, Cela, Delibes, Grosso, Marsé . . . Cómo se hace una novela." *El País Semanal* (Madrid), no. 28 (10 April 1977), pp. 13–15.

Remarks made at Simposio Internacional de Literaturas Hispánicas. University of New Mexico, Albuquerque, New Mexico, 27–29 October 1977.

Interview by John Dyson and Anita Rozlapa. "Entrevista con Juan Benet." *American Hispanist*, 3, no. 22 (December 1977), pp. 19–21.

Remarks made at colloquium on contemporary Spanish literature. Yale University, New Haven, Conn., April 1979.

Remarks made at a colloquium on literature held in Madrid, 29 May 1979. Reported by Juan Cruz in "Batalla literaria en una plaza de Madrid." *El País*, 1 June 1979, p. 27.

"Consideraciones en torno a mi obra." Remarks made at Congreso sobre La Novela Española de Posguerra. San Juan, Puerto Rico, 31 October 1979. (To my knowledge unpublished).

"The Novel in Spain Today: Present State and Future Trends." Remarks made at Spain 1980: An Interdisciplinary Symposium, University of Chicago, 19 April 1980. Published in *La moviola de Eurípides*. Madrid: Taurus, 1982, pp. 23–30.

Interview by Nelson R. Orringer. "Juan Benet a viva voz sobre la filosofía y el ensayo actuales." *Los Ensayistas*, nos. 8–9 (March 1980), pp. 59–65.

Works on Juan Benet *(arranged alphabetically under each heading)*

REVIEWS

Abbott, James H. Review of *Trece fábulas y media. World Literature Today*, 56 (1982), pp. 308–9.

Alfaro, José María. Review of *Un viaje de invierno. ABC*, 25 January 1973, p. 15.

Alonso, Santos. Review of *En el estado. Reseña*, no. 111 (1978), pp. 13–14.

Azancot, Leopoldo. Review of *5 narraciones y 2 fábulas. Estafeta Literaria*, no. 509 (1 February 1973), p. 219.

———. "Juan Benet ante el reto de la democracia." Review of *En el estado. Informaciones de las Artes y las Letras* (supplement to *Informaciones* [Madrid]), no. 475 (25 August 1977), p. 3.

Battló, José. Review of *Volverás a Región. Cuadernos Hispanoamericanos*, no. 299 (January 1969), pp. 234–37.

Benavides, Ricardo. Review of *Una meditación. Books Abroad*, 45 (1977), pp. 285–86.

Cadenas, C. B. "La espera decepcionada." Review of *El aire de un crimen. Nueva Estafeta*, no. 29 (April 1981), pp. 87–88.

Carandell, Luis. "Las claves de Juan Benet." *Diario 16*, 1 November 1981, p. x.

Carrasquer, Francisco. "Un salvavidas." Review of *En el estado. Camp de l'Arpa*, no. 47 (1978), pp. 43–45.

Cerezales, Manuel. Review of *Saúl ante Samuel. ABC*, no. 1598 (August 1980), p. 22.

Chamorro, Eduardo. "La muerte como metáfora." Review of *5 narraciones y 2 fábulas. Triunfo*, no. 539 (1973), pp. 45–46.

———. "Nuevos datos sobre una estética personal." Review of *La otra casa de Mazón. Triunfo*, no. 555 (May 1973), p. 51.

———. "El recuerdo, una partícula incandescente." Review of *Un viaje de invierno. Triunfo*, no. 502 (May 1972).

———. "*Sub rosa* de Juan Benet." *Triunfo*, no. 595 (23 February 1974), pp. 44–45.

Compitello, Malcolm Alan. Review of *Sub rosa. American Hispanist*, 1, no. 3 (November 1976), pp. 17–19.

Conte, Rafael. "La trayectoria de Juan Benet." *Informaciones de las Artes y las Letras* (supplement to *Informaciones* [Madrid]), no. 260 (18 June 1973), pp. 1–2.

———. "Volverás a Juan Benet." Review of *En el estado. El País* (Madrid) *(Suplemento de Arte y Pensamiento)*, no. 35 (1978), p. 1.

———. Review of *El aire de un crimen. El País* (Madrid), *(Suplemento Literario)*, no. 56 (1980), p. 5.

———. "Los límites de Juan Benet." Review of *El aire de un crimen. El País* (Madrid), *(Suplemento Literario)*, 16 November 1980, p. 5.

Correa, Pedro. Review of *Sub Rosa. Nuestro Tiempo*, 41, no. 238 (April 1974), pp. 121–22.

————. "La última novela de Juan Benet." Review of *La otra casa de Mazón*. *Nuestro Tiempo*, 41, no. 235 (January 1974), pp. 95–100.

Cueto, Juan. "Retrato de un novelista de Prado del Rey." *El País* (Madrid) (*Suplemento de Arte y Pensamiento*), no. 1 (16 October 1977), p. xiv.

De La Rosa, Julio M. "Encuentro con Región." *Cuadernos Hispanoamericanos*, no. 369 (1981), pp. 587–92.

Díez Borque, José María. Review of *En ciernes*. *Estafeta Literaria*, no. 599 (1 November 1976), p. 2617.

Domingo, José. "Los caminos de la experimentación: Torrente Ballester, Benet." *Insula*, no. 312 (November 1972), p. 6.

————. "Del hermetismo al barroco: Juan Benet y Alfonso Grosso." *Insula*, nos. 320–321 (July-August 1973), p. 20.

————. "*Una meditación* de Juan Benet." *Insula*, no. 282 (May 1970), p. 7.

————. Review of *Nunca llegarás a nada*. *Insula*, no. 278 (January 1970), p. 5.

Fernández Molina, Antonio. Review of *5 narraciones y 2 fábulas*. *Arbor*, nos. 331–332 (July-August 1973), pp. 170–71.

Franz, Thomas. Review of *La otra casa de Mazón*. *Journal of Spanish Studies: Twentieth Century*, 2, no. 2 (Fall 1974), pp. 197–98.

Gimferrer, Pere. "Los bastidores de Juan Benet." *Destino*, no. 1896 (16 February 1974), p. 31.

————. "Dos rostros de Juan Benet." Review of *5 narraciones y dos fábulas* and *Barojiana*. *Destino*, no. 1844 (February 1973).

————. "Juan Benet, de nuevo en Región." Review of *Una Tumba*. *Triunfo*, no. 475 (November 1971).

————. Review of *Un viaje de invierno*. *Destino*, no. 1820 (August 1972).

————. Review of *Volverás a Región*. *El Ciervo*, no. 179 (January 1969), p. 15.

Gómez Parra, Sergio. Review of *Una meditación*. *Reseña*, no. 42 (1971), pp. 84–85.

————. Review of *Una tumba*. *Reseña*, no. 55 (May 1972), pp. 18–19.

Guelbenzu, José María. "Dos libros de Juan Benet." Review of *Nunca llegarás a nada* and *Volverás a Región*. *Cuadernos para el Diálogo*, no. 73 (October 1969), p. 48.

————. "El paroxismo de lo grotesco." *El País* (Madrid) (*Suplemento de Arte y Pensamiento*), no. 3 (30 October 1977), p. iii.

Gullón, Ricardo. Review of *Sub rosa*. *Journal of Spanish Studies: Twentieth Century*, 3, no. 2 (Fall 1975), pp. 153–54.

Herzberger, David K. "Review of *El ángel del Señor abandona a Tobías*." *American Hispanist*, 2, no. 16 (March 1977), pp. 16–17.

————. Review of *En ciernes*. *American Hispanist*, 1, no. 9 (May 1976), pp. 16–17.

————. Review of *En el estado*. *Anales de la Novela de Posguerra*, 3 (1978), pp. 143–44.

————. Review of *Del pozo y del Numa*. *Anales de la Narrativa Española Contemporánea*, 4 (1979), pp. 176–79.

————. Review of *Un viaje de invierno* by Juan Benet. Edited by Diego Martínez Torrón. *Hispanic Journal*, 3, no. 2 (1982), pp. 129–30.

Iglesias Laguna, Ignacio. Review of *Una meditación*. *ABC* (14 May 1970). Reprinted in Ignacio Iglesias Laguna, *Literatura de España día a día: 1970-1971*. Madrid: Editora Nacional, 1972, pp. 223–27.

Johnson, Roberta. Review of *Sub rosa*. *Books Abroad*, 48 (1975), pp. 743–44.

Josephs, Allen. Review of *A Meditation*. Translated by Gregory Rabassa. *New York Times Book Review*, 23 May 1981, p. 13.

Martí, Octavio. "Las fábulas de Juan Benet." *ABC* (12 January 1973).

Monleón, José. "El teatro de Juan Benet." Article on *Anastas o el origen de la constitución*. *Triunfo*, no. 467 (May 1971), p. 48.

Mora, Manuel R. "Benet en acción." Review of *El aire de un crimen*. *Cambio 16*, no. 470 (1 December 1980), p. 176.

Rebollo Sánchez, Félix. "*Un viaje de invierno* de Juan Benet". Review of Martínez Torrón edition of Benet's novel. *Insula*, no. 422 (1981), p. 7.

Review of *Cuentos completos*. *El País* (Madrid) (*Suplemento de Arte y Pensamiento*), no. 6 (20 November 1977), p. 111.

"Se presentó un aguafuerte de José Guerrero y Juan Benet." *El País* (Madrid), 7 December 1977, p. 27.

Rodríguez Padrón, Jorge. "Volviendo a Región." Review of *5 narraciones y 2 fábulas*. *Camp de l'Arpa*, no. 7 (August-September 1973), pp. 37–38.

Santos Fontanela, F. Review of *Nunca llegarás a nada*. *Insula*, nos. 176–77 (July-August 1971), p. 12.

Schwartz, Kessel. Review of *Saúl ante Samuel*. *Hispania*, 64 (1981), pp. 478–79.

Sordo, Enrique. Review of *Un viaje de invierno*. *Estafeta Literaria*, no. 502 (1972), p. 1108.

————. Review of *Un viaje de invierno*. *El Ciervo*, no. 228 (February 1973), p. 15.

Soto Verges, Rafael. Review of *La inspiración y el estilo*. *Cuadernos Hispanoamericanos*, no. 201 (May 1967), pp. 446–49.

Suñén, Luis. "*El aire de un crimen*." *Insula*, no. 410 (January 1981), pp. 5–6.

————. "*Saúl ante Samuel*." *Insula*, no. 411 (February 1981), p. 5.

————. "Un ejercicio menor de Juan Benet." Review of *Trece fábulas y media*. *El País* (Madrid), (*Suplemento Literario*), no. 89 (5 June 1981), p. 1.

————. "Los pasos de un año discreto." Treats fiction written during 1980 including *Saúl ante Samuel*. *El País* (Madrid), 28 December 1980, p. 5.

Torres Fierro, Danubio. Review of *Del pozo y del Numa*. *Vuelta*, no. 25 (December 1978), pp. 37–39.

Tovar, Antonio. "Juan Benet." *Gaceta Ilustrada*, no. 896 (9 December 1973), p. 34.

Umbral, Franciso. Review of *5 narraciones y 2 fábulas*. *El Urogallo*, nos. 21–22 (May-August 1973), p. 151.

Urbina, Pedro Antonio. Review of *Un viaje de invierno*. *Indice*, no. 310 (July 1972), p. 25.

Valencia, Antonio. Review of *El aire de un crimen*. *Blanco y Negro*, no. 3579 (1980), pp. 53–54.

Valente, José Angel. "Sobre fábulas apólogos y fábulas milesias." Review of *Trece fábulas y media*. *Quimera*, 13 (November 1981), pp. 54–55.

Wiehe, Janet. Review of *A Meditation*. Translated by Gregory Rabassa. *Library Journal*, 1 May 1982, p. 902.

Zulaica, Ramón. "Forever Benet." Review of *El ángel del Señor abandona a Tobías*. *El Diario Vasco* (San Sebastián, Spain), 27 August 1976, p. 10.

STUDIES

Aranguren, José Luis L. "El curso de la novela española contemporánea." Chapter 7 in *Estudios literarios*. Madrid: Gredos, 1976, pp. 213–310.

Aveleyra A., Teresa. "Algo sobre las criaturas de Juan Benet." *Nueva Revista de Filología Hispánica*, 23 (1974), pp. 121–30.

Azúa, Félix de. "El texto invisible. Juan Benet: *Un viaje de invierno*." *Cuadernos de la Gaya Ciencia*, no. 1 (May 1975), pp. 7–21.

Balén, Nora. Ph.D. dissertation dealing with similarities between Benet and Juan Goytisolo. In progress C.U.N.Y. Graduate Center, New York, New York.

Bravo de Regueira, María Elena. "Presencia de Faulkner en España 1933–1973 (su eco en el panorama literario)." Unpublished Ph.D. dissertation. University of Madrid, 1974. Section dealing with relation between Benet and Faulkner to be published in *Prohemio*.

Bravo, María Elena. "Región: una crónica del discurso literario." *MLN*, 98 (1983), pp. 250–58.

Cabrera, Vicente. "El enigma existencial y el sistema de expresión de Benet." Paper delivered at special session on Benet, MLA Convention, New York, N.Y., December 1976.

———. *Juan Benet*. Twayne World Author Series. Boston: G. K. Hall, 1983.

———. "*Volverás a Región*: An Antithetical Pattern of Enigma." Paper delivered at seminar on postwar Spanish novel, MLA Convention, New York, N.Y., December 1975.

Carenas, Francisco, and José Ferrando. "El mundo pre-perceptivo de *Volverás a Región*." In *La sociedad española en la novela de posguerra*, by Francisco Carenas and José Ferrando, New York: Eliseo Torres, 1971, pp. 171–92. Rpt. in *Cuaderno de Norte. Norte: Revista Hispánica de Amsterdam*. Special issue devoted to Agusto Roa Bastos and Juan Benet, 1976, pp. 121–32.

Carrasquer, Francisco. "Brindis." *Cuaderno de Norte. Norte: Revista Hispánica de Amsterdam*. Special issue devoted to Agusto Roa Bastos and Juan Benet, 1976, pp. 73–74.

———. "*Cien años de soledad* y *Volverás a Región*, dos polos." *Norte: Revista Hispánica de Amsterdam*, no. 6 (November-December 1970), pp. 197–201.

Castellet, José María, Pere Gimferrer, and Julián Ríos. "Encuesta: nueva literatura española." *Plural: Revista Mensual de Excelsior*, no. 25 (October 1973), pp. 4–6.

Chamorro, Eduardo. "Intento de aproximación a los textos de Juan Benet." *Cuaderno de Norte. Norte: Revista Hispánica de Amsterdam.* Special issue devoted to Agusto Roa Bastos and Juan Benet, 1976, pp. 110–20.

Compitello, Malcolm Alan. "Juan Benet and the Greeks." Paper delivered at Mountain Interstate Foreign Language Conference, Richmond, Ky., October 1981. Spanish version in press, *Voces* (Barcelona, Spain).

———. "Juan Benet and His Critics." *Anales de la Novela de Posguerra*, 3 (1978), pp. 123–41.

———. "Juan Benet in the Post-War Spanish Novel." Paper delivered at Indiana University, Bloomington, Ind., February 1976.

———. "Juan Benet Scholarship: Some (¿less than?) Modest Proposals." Paper delivered at special session on Benet, MLA Convention, Houston, Tex., December 1980.

———. "Language, Structure, and Ideology in *Volverás a Región.*" *Proceedings of the Fifth Annual Hispanic Literature Conference.* Edited by J. Cruz Mendizábal. Indiana, Pa.: Indiana University of Pennsylvania, 1982, pp. 305–26.

———. "Mythos and Political Community in Juan Benet's *Volverás a Región.*" Paper delivered at Mountain Interstate Foreign Language Conference, Blacksburg, Va., October 1976.

———. "*Volverás a Región*, the Critics, and the Civil War: A Socio-Poetic Reappraisal." *American Hispanist*, 4, no. 36 (May 1979), pp. 11–20.

Díaz, Janet W. "Variations on the Theme of Death in the Short Fiction of Juan Benet." *American Hispanist*, 4, no. 36 (May 1979), pp. 6–11.

———. "Spain's Senior 'New Novelist' Juan Benet." *Studies in Language and Literature. Proceedings of the 23rd Mountain Interstate Foreign Language Conference.* Edited by Charles L. Nelson, Dept. of Foreign Languages, Eastern Kentucky University, Richmond, Ky., 1976, pp. 137–42.

Domingo, José. *La novela española del siglo XX*. vol. 2. Barcelona: Labor, 1973, pp. 156–58.

Durán, Manuel. "Juan Benet y la nueva novela española." *Cuadernos Americanos*, 195, No. 4 (July-August 1974), pp. 193–205.

Fossey, Jean Michel. "Entrevista con Rafael Conte." *Indice*, no. 354 (1974), pp. 33–38. (Contains information pertaining to Benet in context of contemporary Spanish literature).

Gimferrer, Pedro (Pere). "Una crónica de la decadencia." *Papeles de Son Armadans*, no. 156 (March 1969), p. 14.

———. "En torno a *Volverás a Región* de Juan Benet." *Insula*, no. 226 (January 1969), p. 14.

———. "Sobre Juan Benet." *Plural: Revista Mensual de Excelsior*, no. 17 (February 1973), pp. 13–16. Reprinted in a slightly revised version in *Cuaderno de Norte. Norte: Revista Hispánica de Amsterdam.* Special issue devoted to Agusto Roa Bastos and Juan Benet, 1976, pp. 96–109.

Gómez Para, Sergio. "Juan Benet: la ruptura de un horizonte novelístico." *Reseña*, no. 58 (September-October 1971), pp. 3–12.

Guillermo, Edenia, and Juana Amelia Hernández. "Juan Benet. *Volverás a*

*Región.*" In *La novelística española de los sesenta,* by Edenia Guillermo and Juana Amelia Hernández, New York: Eliseo Torres, 1971, pp. 130–50.

Gullón, Ricardo. "Esperando a Coré." *Revista de Occidente,* n.s. no. 145 (April 1975), pp. 16–36.

———. "Una región laberíntica que bien pudiera llamarse España." *Insula,* no. 319 (June 1973), pp. 2, 10.

———. "Sobre espectros y tumbas." *Cuaderno de Norte. Norte: Revista Hispánica de Amsterdam.* Special issue devoted to Agusto Roa Bastos and Juan Benet, 1976, pp. 83–95.

———. "Introducción." In *Una tumba y otros relatos,* by Juan Benet. Madrid: Taurus, 1981, pp. 7–50.

Herzberger, David K. "The Emergence of Juan Benet: A New Alternative for the Spanish Novel." *American Hispanist,* 1, no. 3 (November 1975), pp. 6–12.

———. "Enigma as Narrative Determinant in the Novels of Juan Benet." *Hispanic Review,* 47 (1979), pp. 149–57.

———. "Juan Benet's *Una tumba.*" *American Hispanist,* 1, no. 9 (May 1976), pp. 3–6.

———. "Novelists on the Novel: The Theoretical Disparity of Contemporary Spanish Narrative." *Symposium,* 33 (1979), pp. 215–29.

———. *The Novelistic World of Juan Benet.* Clear Creek, Ind.: American Hispanist, 1976.

———. "Some Freudian Principles in the Novels of Juan Benet." Unpublished paper.

———. "Style and Enigma in Benet's Theory of the Novel." Paper delivered at special session on Benet, MLA Convention, New York, N.Y., December 1976.

———. "Theoretical Approaches to the Spanish New Novel: Juan Benet and Juan Goytisolo. *Revista de Estudios Hispánicos,* 14, no. 2 (May 1980), pp. 3–17.

Ionescu, Andrei. "Explorarea unui spatiu mitic." *Seculol XX,* nos. 166–167 (1974), pp. 87–92.

"Juan Benet en la Fundación March." *ABC,* 6 June 1975, p. 39.

Mangini González, Shirley. "El punto de vista dual en tres novelistas españoles." *Insula,* nos. 396–397 (November-December 1979), pp. 7, 9.

Manteiga, Roberto C. "Benet Ventures Beyond Región." *Denver Quarterly,* 17, no. 3 (Fall 1982), pp. 76–82.

———. "*En el estado*: Benet Ventures Beyond Región." Paper delivered at the Louisiana Conference on Hispanic Languages and Literatures, Tulane University, New Orleans, La., February 26–28, 1981.

———. "Trapped in Time: The Ideas of Doomed Repetition and Forboding Prophecy in Juan Benet's Short Fiction". Paper delivered at the Louisiana Conference on Hispanic Languages and Literatures, Louisiana State University, Baton Rouge, La., February 18–20, 1982.

Marco, Joaquín. "La novela de un escritor." *Destino,* 29 June 1968, p. 34. Reprinted in *Ejercicios literarios,* by Joaquín Marco. Barcelona: Taber, 1969, pp. 291–96.

164 Bibliography

4 Bibliography

————. "Las obras recientes de Juan Benet." In *Nueva literatura en España y América*, by Joaquín Marco. Barcelona: Lumen, 1972, pp. 143–55.
Marín Morales, J. A. "'Puerta de tierra,' de Juan Benet." *Arbor*, nos. 295–296 (July-August 1970), pp. 135–38.
Martínez-Lázaro, Marisa. "Juan Benet o la incertidumbre como fundamento." *El Urogallo*, nos. 11–12 (September-December 1971), pp. 175–76.
Martínez Torrón, Diego. "Juan Benet o los márgenes de la sorpresa." In *Un viaje de invierno*, by Juan Benet. Edited by Diego Martínez Torrón. Madrid: Cátedra, 1980, pp. 11–110.
Montero, Isaac. "Acotaciones a una mesa redonda: respuestas a Juan Benet y defensa apresurada del realismo." *Cuadernos para el Diálogo*, special issue, 23 (December 1970), pp. 65–74.
————. "La novela española de 1955 hasta hoy: una crisis de dos exaltaciones antagónicas." *Triunfo*, special issue, 507 (17 June 1972), pp. 86–94.
Nelson, Esther W. "The Aesthetics of Refraction: A Comparative Study of *Pedro Páramo* and *Volverás a Región*." Paper delivered at special session on Benet, MLA Convention, Chicago, Ill., December 1977.
————. "Narrative Perspective in *Volverás a Región*." *American Hispanist*, 4, no. 36 (May 1979), pp. 3–6.
Noles, Ludovico. "Adiós a Región (Una entrevista con Juan Benet)." *Quimera*, no. 3 (January 1981), pp. 9–15.
Oliart, Alberto. "Viaje a Región." *Revista de Occidente*, n.s. no. 80 (November 1969), pp. 224–34. Reprint. *Novelistas españoles de posguerra*, edited by Rodolfo Cardona. Madrid: Taurus, 1976, pp. 185–94.
Ortega, José. "Estudios sobre la obra de Juan Benet." *Cuadernos Hispanoamericanos*, no. 284 (February 1974), pp. 229–58. Reprint. Ensayos de la novela española moderna, by José Ortega. Madrid: José Porrúa Turanzas, 1974, pp. 137–77.
————. "Tres fichas sobre Benet: *La otra casa de Mazón, Una tumba, Sub rosa*." In his *Ultimas direcciones de la novelística española contemporánea*. Madrid: José Porrúa Turanzas, in press.
Overesch, Lynn. Ph.D. dissertation on neo-baroque narrative in Spain, University of Kentucky, 1981.
Rodríguez Padrón, Jorge. "Apuntes para una teoría benetiana." *Insula*, nos. 396–397 (November-December 1979), pp. 3, 5.
Sandarg, Jana. "The Role of Nature in the Novels of Región". Ph.D. dissertation, University of North Carolina, Chapel Hill, 1980.
Sanz Villanueva, Santos. *Tendencias de la novela española actual (1950-1970)*. Madrid: Cuadernos para el Diálogo, 1972, pp. 179–82.
Schwartz, Ronald. "Benet and *Volverás a Región* 1967." Chapter 17 in *Spain's New Wave Novelists 1959-1974. Studies in Spanish Realism*. Metuchen, N.J.: Scarecrow Press, 1976, pp. 233–44.
Sobejano, Gonzalo. "Estructuras enigmáticas." In *Cuentos Españoles Concertados. De Clarín a Benet*. Edited by Gonzalo Sobejano and Gary D. Keller. New York: Harcourt Brace Jovanovich, 1975, pp. 245–49.

————. *Novela española de nuestro tiempo: en busca del pueblo perdido.* Madrid: Prensa Española, 1970, pp. 401–7.

————. "La novela estructural: de Luis Martín-Santos a Juan Benet." Chapter 13 in *Novela española de nuestro tiempo: en busca del pueblo perdido*, 2d ed. Madrid: Prensa Española, 1975, pp. 545–609.

Solomon, Barbara Probst. *Los felices cuarenta: una educación sentimental.* Barcelona: Seix Barral, 1978. Translation of her autobiographical novel *Arriving Where We Started* (New York: Harper and Row, 1972) that contains important biographical information on Benet and his family.

Spires, Robert C. "*Volverás a Región* y la desintegración total." In *La novela española de posguerra.* Madrid: Cupsa Editorial, 1978, pp. 224–46.

Summerhill, Stephen J. "Prohibition and Transgression in Juan Benet." *American Hispanist*, 4, no. 36 (May 1979), pp. 20–24.

Thomas, Michael Duane. "Myth and Archetype in the New Spanish Novel (1950–1970): A Study in Changing Novelistic Techniques." *Dissertation Abstracts International*, 37 (1976), p. 1013-A.

Torres Fierro, Danubio. "Juan Benet: La inspiración y el estilo." In *Los territorios del exilio.* Barcelona: La Gaya Ciencia, 1979, pp. 153–58. (On *Del pozo y del Numa*).

Vásquez, Mary S. "Taking the Measure of the Past: Existential Self-Creation in Benet's *Una meditación.*" Paper presented at Rocky Mountain Modern Language Association Convention, Albuquerque, N. Mex., October 1979.

————. "The Creative Task: Existential Self-Invention in Benet's *Una meditación.*" *Selecta*, no. 1 (1980), pp. 118–20.

Vernon, Kathleen. "Amor, fantasía, vacío en un cuento de Juan Benet." *Insula*, no. 410 (January 1981), pp. 1, 10.

Villanueva, Darío. "La novela de Juan Benet." *Camp de l'Arpa*, no. 8 (November 1973), pp. 9–16.

————. Presentation on Benet's narrative made during the Coloquio sobre Novela Española Actual at Fundación Juan March, 2–7 June 1975. Published as "Las narraciones de Juan Benet," in *Novela española actual*, edited by Andrés Amorós. Madrid: Fundación Juan March/Editorial Cátedra, 1977, pp. 133–72.

Wescott, Julia L. "Creation and Structure of Enigma: Literary Conventions and Juan Benet's Trilogy." Ph.D. dissertation, University of Massachusetts, 1982.

————. "Exposition and Plot in Benet's *Volverás a Región.*" *Kentucky Romance Quarterly*, 28 (1981), pp. 155–63.

Yerro Villanueva, Tomás. *Aspectos técnicos y estructurales de la novela española actual.* Pamplona: Editorial de la Universidad de Pamplona, 1977.

Zoetmulder, Ingrid. "Provisional bibliografía benetiana." *Cuaderno de Norte. Norte: Revista Hispánica de Amsterdam.* Special issue devoted to Agusto Roa Bastos and Juan Benet, 1976, pp. 133–40.

# Contributors

Robert C. Spires is Professor of Spanish at the University of Kansas. He is the author of *La novela española de posguerra* and numerous articles on twentieth-century Spanish literature.

Malcolm Alan Compitello is the author of *Ordering the Evidence*: *Volverás a Región and Civil War Fiction*, as well as several articles on the contemporary Spanish novel. He is Associate Professor of Spanish at Michigan State University.

Janet Pérez is the author of several books and articles on twentieth-century Spanish literature. She is Professor of Spanish at Texas Tech University.

Esther W. Nelson has written on the contemporary literature of both Spain and Latin America. She is currently Assistant Professor of Spanish at the University of Southern California.

Nelson R. Orringer is Professor of Spanish at the University of Connecticut. He is the author of *Ortega y sus fuentes germánicas* and *Unamuno y su teología* and has written numerous articles on twentieth-century Spanish literature and philosophy.

Stephen J. Summerhill is Associate Professor of Spanish at Ohio State University. He has written primarily on twentieth-century Spanish narrative and poetry.

Mary S. Vásquez is Associate Professor of Spanish at Arizona State University. She has published numerous studies on both contemporary Spanish and Hispanic-American literature and is the author of *Weaver of Clay*, a collection of original poems.

Julia Lupinacci Wescott received her doctorate in Spanish from the University of Massachusetts, where she wrote her dissertation on Juan Benet. She currently teaches Spanish at The Nichols School in Buffalo, N.Y.

Gonzalo Díaz-Migoyo is Assistant Professor of Spanish at the University of Texas. He is the author of a monograph on *El bus-*

*cón* and numerous articles on Golden Age and modern Spanish literature.

David K. Herzberger is Associate Professor of Spanish at the University of Connecticut. He is the author of *The Novelistic World of Juan Benet* and *Jesús Fernández Santos* and has written extensively on contemporary Spanish narrative.

Randolph D. Pope is Chairman of the Department of Hispanic Studies at Vassar College. He has published extensively in many areas of Hispanic literature.

Roberto C. Manteiga is Associate Professor of Hispanic Studies at the University of Rhode Island. He is author of *The Poetry of Rafael Alberti: A Visual Approach* and has published numerous articles on contemporary Spanish poetry and narrative.

# Index